SECOND EDITION

Copyright Law for Librarians and Educators

Creative Strategies and Practical Solutions

KENNETH D. CREWS

A Project of the Copyright Management Center
Indiana University–Purdue University Indianapolis

WITH CONTRIBUTIONS FROM

Dwayne K. Buttler

Megan M. Mulford

Patrick O. Okorodudu

Jacque M. Ramos

Joshua S. Sullivan

David A. W. Wong

American Library Association

Chicago   2006

Printed on 50-pound white offset, a pH-neutral stock, and bound in 10-point cover stock by McNaughton & Gunn.

The paper used in this publication meets the minimum requirements of American National Standard for Information Sciences—Permanence of Paper for Printed Library Materials, ANSI Z39.48-1992. ∞

Library of Congress Cataloging-in-Publication Data

Crews, Kenneth D.
    Copyright law for librarians and educators : creative strategies and practical solutions / Kenneth D. Crews.—2nd ed.
        p.   cm.
    Rev. ed. of: Copyright essentials for librarians and educators. 2000.
    Includes bibliographical references and index.
    0-8389-0906-X
    1. Copyright—United States. 2. Librarians—United States—Handbooks, manuals, etc. 3. Teachers—United States—Handbooks, manuals, etc.
    4. Fair use (Copyright)—United States. I. Crews, Kenneth D. Copyright essentials for librarians and educators. II. Title.

    KF2995.C74 2005
    346.7304'82'02402—dc   2005013804

Printed in the United States of America

09   08   07   06   05   5   4   3   2   1

In celebration of the life of
Dr. John Allen Gable, PhD,
1943–2005,
Executive Director,
Theodore Roosevelt Association,
and good friend

CONTENTS

APPENDIXES

INTRODUCTION:
This Book and the Importance of Copyright

THE RELATIONSHIP BETWEEN COPYRIGHT LAW AND THE PURSUIT OF innovative education, librarianship, and scholarship has become more important and more complex in recent years. New legislation from Congress attempts to redefine the use of copyrighted materials in distance education, whether by television broadcasts or over electronic networks. Courts have elaborated on critical questions of fair use. Judicial rulings continue to give new insights into the meaning of the Digital Millennium Copyright Act, a new law which may determine access to a wealth of essential research sources. In addition, the question of "who owns" the copyright to new works has become one of the most troublesome copyright questions at colleges and universities.

Even if copyright law never changed, the activities of educators and librarians have been transformed. We steadily digitize and upload diverse materials. We launch websites for every program and project. We download materials from databases and manipulate and incorporate them into online instruction. Our understanding of copyright and our ability to work with the law can make these important endeavors more successful.

Objectives of This Book

The primary purpose of this book is to examine the copyright issues of central importance to education, librarianship, and scholarship. Readers will see immediately that the fundamentals of copyright make the law crucial to our diverse activities. Copyright law bestows automatic protection for printed works, software, art, websites, and nearly everything else we create and use in our teaching and research. The protection lasts for decades, and we can infringe the copyright with simple photocopying or elaborate scanning and uploading.

Fortunately, copyright law includes a number of exceptions to owners' rights, such as "fair use." Several other detailed provisions of the U.S. Copyright Act specifically benefit education and learning. These provisions allow library copying, permit performances and displays in classrooms or in distance learning, and sanction backup copies of computer software. This book will acquaint readers with the vital role these exceptions play in the functioning of copyright and in the growth of knowledge. This book also offers strategies and techniques for reaping the benefits of these rights of use.

Taking Control

As professionals in the world of education and librarianship, we can enjoy the law's benefits only if we understand the rules of the copyright world. We must comprehend our rights as owners and as users. We ultimately need to identify alternatives that the law allows and make decisions about copyright that best advance our objectives as teachers, learners, and information professionals. If we do not manage copyright to our advantage, we will lose valuable opportunities for achieving our teaching and research missions.

This book demonstrates that understanding and applying much of copyright law is within the reach of professionals with diverse backgrounds. Admittedly, some aspects of the law will be bewildering and occasionally unworkable. But most issues about ownership, publication, library services, and fair use are manageable, and we can make practical sense of them. Copyright does not have to be an annoying or threatening beast that merely burdens your work. With a fresh understanding of the law, it can actually support teachers and scholars who are striving to meet their goals each day.

Origin of This Book

This book has several origins. It is a full revision and restructuring of *Copyright Essentials for Librarians and Educators,* written by the same author and published in 2000 by ALA Editions. This restructured book gives greater focus to major issues that have emerged in recent years, such as complications surrounding music, online networks, and changes in the law of fair use. The revisions are sometimes updates or a complete recasting of explanations of the law. Nearly every piece of the original book was reworked to make copyright clearer and more meaningful to the reader. Not a single sentence from the earlier book made its way into this book without a fresh evaluation and usually a significant rewrite. Indeed, whole chapters and other lengthy portions of this book are entirely new.

This book and the earlier version have been projects of the Copyright Management Center (CMC) at Indiana University–Purdue University Indianapolis (IUPUI). The CMC has a primary mission of addressing copyright issues of importance to education and research, and readers may find a variety of helpful materials at http://www.copyright.iupui.edu. Some readers may fondly recall the "Online Copyright Tutorial" offered by the CMC in the 1990s. Those online messages were the direct precursor of the 2000 book, and they remain an inspiration for this new publication. Some modest pieces of this book can be traced to a few of the author's earlier projects. One was a general study of fair use developed for California State University. Another project was a guide for graduate students writing dissertations, and it is available from ProQuest Information and Learning. With updates and rewriting, however, relatively little of those earlier works is included here verbatim.

Acknowledgments

The author personally reworked every detail of this book, but completing it would not have been possible without important contributions from several great colleagues and associates. I am especially pleased to acknowledge Dwayne K. Buttler, my former colleague at IUPUI, who now holds a position with copyright responsibilities at the University of Louisville. Dwayne was instrumental in creating the original book, and he was critical to this new book as well. I have been gifted with the support of three outstanding students from the Indiana University School of Law–Indianapolis. David A. W. Wong (class of 2004) and Megan M. Mulford (class of 2005) worked with the entire manuscript, made various important contributions, and questioned my statements at every stage. Joshua S. Sullivan, administrative assistant to the Copyright Management Center, kept the project organized and progressing.

I designated Jacque M. Ramos (class of 2005) as "project manager" to keep this project on track and to test and scrutinize every detail of it. Jacque brought profound intuition and organizational skills to the task. She planned each step and constantly—and courteously—returned to me anything that did not pass her judgment. Much of the shape and content of this book are due to the critical and intelligent perspective that Jacque offered each day with enthusiasm and care. Bobak Jalaie (class of 2007) joined the project in the final stages and helped refine details throughout.

I continue to thank Dr. William M. Plater, executive vice chancellor of IUPUI. His vision led to the creation of the CMC in 1994, and his steady support has undergirded all of our efforts. I give unending thanks to my wife, Elizabeth, and to my children, Veronica and Will, who tolerated my long hours at work and late nights at the computer. I extend special thanks to the national network of friends and associates who have appreciated my life spent with copyright, who have come to the well for a little guidance now and again, and who have invited me to visit their colleges, universities, and libraries. The enthusiasm of my readers has inspired this book and continues to motivate all my efforts when the burden sometimes seems overwhelming.

Kenneth D. Crews

1

The Scope of Protectable Works

KEY POINTS

- A work must be both "original" and "fixed in any tangible medium of expression" to be copyrightable.

- "Originality" requires a minimum amount of creativity.

- A work is "fixed" if it is embodied in some stable form for more than a brief duration.

- A "tangible medium" allows a work to be perceived or communicated.

The U.S. Copyright Act sets forth in Section 102(a) that copyright protection vests immediately and automatically upon the creation of "original works of authorship" that are "fixed in any tangible medium of expression."[1]

Originality

Fundamentally, "originality" in copyright law means that the work came from your inspiration, and that you did not copy it from another source. Originality also implies some creativity. Originality is easily found in new writings, musical works, artworks, photography, and computer programming. You may also find originality in a new arrangement of existing facts or information. Scientific findings or facts may not themselves be copyrightable, but their arrangement in a table or their presentation in text may be protectable expression.

Based upon this principle, the content and layout of most websites are certainly copyrightable. The text, images, and other elements in them are often original works. Decisions about the placement of text and photos, the selection of information on the website, and how users will access the site could easily be "original," rendering the website protectable under the law.

Similarly, Homer's epic poems may never have had any legal protection under the laws of ancient Greece, but a new translation is an "original" work subject to new copyright protection as a "derivative." A derivative work takes the original work, for example *The Iliad,* and creates a new work from it—such as a translation into a different language, a motion picture, a stage play, a musical, an interactive website, or numerous other possibilities. Hollywood studios can create *Troy* and hold rights to it, while the original book remains in the public domain.

Creativity and Originality

How much "originality" is required? An original work must embody some *minimum amount of creativity.* Courts have held that almost any spark of creativity beyond the "trivial" will constitute sufficient originality. The U.S. Supreme Court ruled in 1991 that a "garden-variety," alphabetical, white-pages telephone book lacks the requisite minimum creativity for copyright protection.[2] Cases since 1991 have affirmed this ruling, but have tested its limits. For example, a yellow-pages listing may have sufficient originality resulting from its categorization of information under subject headings.[3]

> "There is nothing remotely creative about arranging names alphabetically in a white pages directory."
>
> —U.S. Supreme Court Justice Sandra Day O'Connor in *Feist Publications, Inc. v. Rural Telephone Service Co.*

Long ago, the Supreme Court faced similar questions about a photograph of Oscar Wilde. The Supreme Court held that the picture met the standard of creativity because the photographer chose the camera, equipment, lighting, angles, and placement of the subject when shooting the picture.[4] More recently, however, a federal court has ruled that a direct, accurate photographic reproduction of a two-dimensional artwork lacks sufficient creativity to be original.[5] The work of art may still be creative and

Photograph of Oscar Wilde by Napoleon Sarony, 1882

Courtesy of University of California, Los Angeles

> "[The photograph is] entirely from [the photographer's] own original mental conception . . . by posing . . . Wilde . . ., selecting and arranging the costume, draperies, and other various accessories in said photograph, arranging the subject so as to present graceful outlines, arranging and disposing the light and shade, suggesting and evoking the desired expression."
>
> —U.S. Supreme Court Justice Samuel Miller in *Burrow-Giles Lithographic Co. v. Sarony*

protected by copyright, but not the simple and direct photographic reproduction of it. As in the Oscar Wilde case, should the photograph of the artwork include creative lighting, coloring, or angles, or capture more than just the work of art itself, then the photograph could easily qualify for copyright protection.

> Copyright protection is based on a recognition of creativity, not hard work. A court recently denied copyright protection for photographic copies of art. Although acknowledging that the photography required great technical skill, the court still called it "slavish copying."
>
> —*Bridgeman Art Library, Ltd. v. Corel Corp.,* 36 F. Supp. 2d 191 (S.D.N.Y. 1999)

Fixed in a Tangible Medium

For an "original work of authorship" to be eligible for copyright protection, it must also be "fixed" in some physical form capable of identification that exists for more than a "transitory duration."[6] Examples of "fixed" works might include scribbles on paper, recordings of music, paintings on canvas, and documents on web servers.

The fixed form does not have to be readable by the human eye, as long as the work can be perceived either directly or by a machine or device, such as a computer or projector.[7] Therefore, programming and substantive content stored on floppy disks or CDs are "fixed," as long as the works can be read with the use of a machine.

Expansion of Copyrightability

The "tangible medium" requirement expands copyright from traditional writings and pictures into the realm of video, sound recordings, computer disks, and Internet communications—any format now known or to be later developed.[8] If you can see it, read it, watch it, or hear it—with or without the use of a computer, projector, or other machine—the work is likely eligible for copyright protection. Harder questions surround whether materials stored only in the random-access memory (RAM) of a computer are sufficiently "fixed" to be eligible for protection. A fleeting appearance in RAM may not be enough, but once you hit the print or save key, that work is easily within the purview of copyright.

> An important court case held that software programming loaded into RAM was sufficiently stable to qualify as a "copy" for purposes of establishing an infringement. The concept of a work in a stable medium for purposes of copying is similar to the standard used to determine if the work is "fixed" in the first place to establish copyright protection.
>
> —*MAI Systems Corp.*
> *v. Peak Computer, Inc.,*
> 991 F.2d 511 (9th Cir. 1993)

Given the wide range of media and nearly boundless scope of "originality," the result is a vast array of works brought under copyright protection. In addition, the statutes list various categories of works that are generally protectable. Section 102(a) of the Copyright Act specifies that copyrightable works can include these categories:[9]

- Literary works
- Musical works, including any accompanying words
- Dramatic works, including any accompanying music
- Pantomimes and choreographic works
- Pictorial, graphic, and sculptural works
- Motion pictures and other audiovisual works
- Sound recordings
- Architectural works

These categories are illustrative and are not exhaustive of all possibilities. Because the categories are construed liberally, "literary works" can range from novels to computer programs. The category of "pictorial" or "graphic" works can include maps, charts, and other visual imagery.[10]

Because of the law's vast reach, the important question may not be what *is* copyrightable, but what is *not* copyrightable. The next chapter will identify various types of works that are without copyright protection.

Notes

1. *U.S. Copyright Act*, 17 *U.S.C.* § 102(a) (2005).
2. *Feist Publications, Inc. v. Rural Telephone Service Co.*, 499 U.S. 340 (1991).
3. *Bellsouth Advertising & Publishing Corp. v. Donnelley Information Publishing, Inc.*, 999 F.2d 1436 (11th Cir. 1993).
4. *Burrow-Giles Lithographic Co. v. Sarony*, 111 U.S. 53 (1884).
5. *Bridgeman Art Library, Ltd. v. Corel Corp.*, 36 F. Supp. 2d 191 (S.D.N.Y. 1999).
6. The word *fixed*, as well as many other terms, is defined in the copyright statutes. *U.S. Copyright Act*, 17 *U.S.C.* § 101 (2005).
7. *U.S. Copyright Act*, 17 *U.S.C.* § 102(a) (2005).
8. *U.S. Copyright Act*, 17 *U.S.C.* § 102(a).
9. *U.S. Copyright Act*, 17 *U.S.C.* § 102(a).
10. *U.S. Copyright Act*, 17 *U.S.C.* § 101.

2

Works without Copyright Protection

KEY POINTS

■ Ideas and facts are not protected by copyright.

■ Works of the U.S. government are not copyrightable, but works created by state or local governments may be protected.

■ Other specific types of works may be outside of copyright protection, such as databases, but future legislation may grant protection.

■ Once a copyright has expired, the work is no longer protected by copyright law and it enters the public domain.

While copyright protection applies broadly to expressions that are "original" and "fixed," several categories of works are specifically outside the boundaries of the law. These works are wholly without copyright protection, are in the public domain, and are freely available for use without copyright restrictions. For example, ideas are not protectable.[1] If you tell a friend your great idea for a book or scientific breakthrough, and she uses only the idea in her own work, you have no copyright claim. You may certainly find an ethical violation, or possibly a breach of other legal rights, but copyright simply does not protect ideas alone.[2]

Many works are without copyright protection for good reason. The law grants rights for many reasons, perhaps most notably to encourage creativity and the dissemination of new works. Sometimes limiting or denying rights also serves an important purpose. If ideas were protectable, we might be left with only one version of a story, one software package for each need, or only one work of art that expresses beauty or angst. Sometimes denying rights can better foster creativity and render the greatest benefit for individuals and for society in general.

> Recall from chapter 1 that for works to be afforded copyright protection, they must be "original" works of authorship and "fixed" in a tangible medium of expression.
>
> —*U.S. Copyright Act*, 17 *U.S.C.* § 102(a) (2005)

Facts and Discoveries

Facts and discoveries are also not protectable by copyright.[3] Facts cannot by definition be "original" as the law requires. You may conduct years of creative scientific study to discover a *fact* about the universe, but the fact itself is not *your* creative work. Denying legal protection for facts also assures that everyone can build on existing knowledge and share information.

On the other hand, you may have copyright protection for your original *compilations of facts* or your *writings about the facts and discoveries*.[4] For example, after years of research to find facts, you write a journal article about your research findings. The sentences and paragraphs are most surely creative, original, and protectable. Suppose your article also includes several tables that organize the facts in a manner that is meaningful to your readers. For example, you might chart the boiling point of water, the rate of urban crime, or the election of presidents. To the extent that you have selected, arranged, or coordinated the facts in some original manner, you can claim a "compilation copyright" in the presentation. Still, the facts are not your intellectual property. Another writer can extract the facts and include them in a new study.

> The U.S. Supreme Court has made clear that copyright protection depends on creativity, but the measure of creativity is modest at best. According to the Court, the "requisite level of creativity is extremely low; even a slight amount will suffice. The vast majority of works make the grade quite easily, as they possess some creative spark, 'no matter how crude, humble or obvious' it might be."
>
> —*Feist Publications, Inc. v. Rural Telephone Service Co.*, 499 U.S. 340 (1991)

Compilations and Databases

Copyright law may not protect everything, but the law can protect original "compilations" of otherwise unprotected material. Real examples of compilation copyrights are common. For example, many companies create and publish bibliographies and other compilations of information. Individual author names, article titles, and the like are not protected, but the original arrangement of them into useful research resources can be protected.[5] Similarly, an editor may select your article for publication and arrange it with other selections into a new journal issue. You may still hold the copyright for your individual work, but the editor can hold a copyright in the compilation of the overall journal issue.[6]

> You might write poetry in your spare time. You can have copyright protection for each poem. After some years of writing, you gather the poems, arrange them into a logical or interesting order, and publish the collection as a book. You can have an additional copyright in the original compilation. You can even have a "compilation copyright" if you collect the poems of other authors.

Not all compilations of information are protected. Databases have copyright protection only if they are original in their selection, arrangement, or coordination of data elements. Selecting and organizing articles in a journal usually involve considerable originality. Gathering data and listing it alphabetically or chronologically, or just uploading it in no order into a computer, often involve no creativity. Without creativity, there can be no copyright protection. The lack of protection for many databases causes great concern for companies that invest significantly to develop and market such works. In recent years, Congress has considered new legislation that would establish a new form of legal protection for data compilations. Many educators and librarians have cautioned against these bills, arguing that such a law would further restrain access to information.

> Revealing the split in Congress over the wisdom of database protection, two bills on this topic were recently introduced into Congress. The bills represent sharply divergent views about the appropriate means of protection, the strength of owner rights, and the scope of exceptions. These bills are the *Consumer Access to Information Act*, HR 3872, 108th Cong., 2d sess. (2004); and the *Database and Collections of Information Misappropriation Act*, HR 3261, 108th Cong., 1st sess. (2003).

All of these examples underscore the need to distinguish between the various elements of a total work, and to establish carefully whether each element is copyrightable. Some elements may be in the public domain. Some elements may be separately copyrighted and held by different owners. Sometimes the distinction between them is easy to see, such as the difference between the article and the journal. In other instances, the distinction between uncopyrightable materials and protectable creativity is less clear.

A biography of Benjamin Franklin is easily protectable, but the facts stated in the text are not. A book about rare coins is also protectable, but the stated value of each coin may be a "fact" about market prices—or not. If the price is simply a recent actual selling price, it is likely a "fact." On the other hand, one court has ruled that wholesale prices for collectible coins based on multivariable judgment calls and the appraiser's "best guess" are creative works protectable under copyright.[7]

Works of the U.S. Government

The United States government produces numerous works that may be "original" and "fixed," but that are still not copyrightable. Section 105 of the U.S. Copyright Act specifically prohibits copyright protection for works of the federal government.[8] Therefore, reports written by members of Congress and employees of federal agencies, as part of their official duties, are not copyrightable. Decisions from federal courts and statutes from Congress are not protected. The same holds true for presidential speeches, pamphlets from the National Park Service, and websites developed by federal agencies.[9]

Even this broad rule of copyright is not as simple as it seems. Projects written by nongovernment officials with federal funding may be copyrightable. For example, your research may be funded by government grants; that fact does not by itself put your work in the public domain. A government-funded project is not necessarily a "work of the United States Government."

Similarly, just because a work is published by the federal government does not mean that it is a government work and in the public domain. A publication from the Smithsonian Institution, for example, may well have been prepared by nongovernment authors and is therefore protectable by copyright. A brochure from the National Park Service may include copyrighted photographs licensed from an independent photographer. You need to examine each item closely, and inquire with the author or the issuing agency if you are in doubt.

> A bill recently introduced in the state legislature of California would have prohibited the state from asserting rights to intellectual property, and it would have dedicated to the public domain most copyrights that might have been held by the state. The bill is *2003 California Assembly Bill No. 1616* (2003–2004, introduced on February 21, 2003, amended on February 2, 2004).

Keep in mind that this exemption applies only to works of the United States federal government. Works created by state and local governments are protected by copyright unless those governments have expressly waived their claims of copyright by statute. Some states have gone in the other direction. The Idaho legislature has provided a blunt and direct declaration about copyright for its statutes: "The Idaho Code is the property of the state of Idaho, and the state of Idaho and the taxpayers shall be deemed to have a copyright on the Idaho Code."[10] Inquire with the appropriate state agency about possible copyright protection for its materials.

> Additional works may be in the public domain for a variety of reasons. An author may voluntarily choose to dedicate a work to the public domain. The law has in the past recognized a concept of "abandonment" of a copyright. Sometimes Congress has simply chosen not to extend copyright to all works. For example, sound recordings are protectable today, but U.S. recordings made before Congress changed the law, effective February 15, 1972, are without copyright protection. Chapter 14 offers much more information about copyright and sound recordings.

Outside the Reach of Copyright

Several additional categories of material are generally not eligible for statutory copyright protection:

- Works that have not been fixed in a tangible form of expression. Examples include choreographic works that have not been noted or recorded, and improvisational speeches or performances that have not been written or recorded.

- Titles, names, short phrases, and slogans, as well as familiar symbols or designs— although the law of trademark may offer some protection[11]

- Mere variations of typographic ornamentation, lettering, or coloring; mere listings of ingredients, as in recipes, or contents[12]

- Ideas, procedures, methods, systems, processes, concepts, principles, discoveries, or devices.[13] On the other hand, patent or trade secret law may offer protection for some of these works.

- Works consisting entirely of information that is common property and containing no original authorship. Examples include standard calendars, height and weight charts, tape measures and rulers, and lists or tables taken from public documents or other common sources.

Expired Copyrights

Another important source of the public domain is the expiration of copyright for any work. Copyrights may last a long time, but they do expire after a set number of years. Consequently, works that may have been protected in the past may have lost their copyright due to the age of the work. The copyright to works from before 1989 may also have expired due to failure to comply with "formalities" that were once required. The next chapter of this book takes a close look at the duration of copyright protection and the process of identifying works in the public domain.

Notes

1. *U.S. Copyright Act*, 17 *U.S.C.* § 102(b) (2005).
2. An example of a legal doctrine that might come into play in such a situation could be "misappropriation." See *NXIVM Corp. v. Ross Institute*, 364 F.3d 471 (2d Cir. 2004); *Gaiman v. McFarlane*, 360 F.3d 644 (7th Cir. 2004); *Brown v. Ames*, 201 F.3d 654 (5th Cir. 2000).

3. *U.S. Copyright Act*, 17 *U.S.C.* § 102(b).

4. *Silverstein v. Penguin Putnam, Inc.*, 368 F.3d 77 (2d Cir. 2005); *Feist Publications, Inc. v. Rural Telephone Service Co.*, 499 U.S. 340 (1991).

5. *Code of Federal Regulations*, title 37, vol.1, sec. 202.1 (2005).

6. Section 201(c) of the U.S. Copyright Act states: "Copyright in each separate contribution to a collective work is distinct from copyright in the collective work as a whole."

7. *CDN Inc. v. Kapes*, 197 F.3d 1256 (9th Cir. 1999).

8. *U.S. Copyright Act*, 17 *U.S.C.* § 105 (2005).

9. The U.S. Copyright Act defines a "work of the United States Government" as "a work prepared by an officer or employee of the United States Government as part of that person's official duties." *U.S. Copyright Act*, 17 *U.S.C.* § 101 (2005). For an example of the application of this rule to court opinions, see *Matthew Bender & Co. v. West Publishing Co.*, 158 F.3d 693 (2d Cir. 1998).

10. *Idaho Code*, sec. 9-350 (Matthew Bender, 2004).

11. *Code of Federal Regulations*, title 37, vol. 1, sec. 202.1.

12. *Code of Federal Regulations*, title 37, vol. 1, sec. 202.1.

13. *U.S. Copyright Act*, 17 *U.S.C.* § 102(b) (2005).

PART II ■ Rights of Ownership

3 Duration and Formalities:
How Long Do Copyrights Last?

KEY POINTS

- Current law no longer requires the formalities of notice or registration for copyright protection.

- Most new works are protected for the life of the author plus seventy years.

- Works published before 1978 were required to have a copyright notice in order to gain protection.

- Works published between 1923 and 1978 could have protection for up to ninety-five years.

- Many foreign works that were in the public domain have had their copyrights restored.

Copyrights do not last forever. They may last a long time, or they may expire in relatively short order. Either way, the question of copyright "duration" can be both enormously controversial and unduly complicated. The duration of copyright is important because it signals when a work will enter the "public domain" and become available for use, free of the limits and restrictions of copyright law. The number of years of protection a work receives under the law can depend on many facts and variables.

Under today's law, copyright duration for current works is relatively uncomplicated. Copyrights to most new works last throughout the author's life, plus seventy more years.[1] These rights vest for the full term automatically without the need to undertake any processes or procedures.[2] For works created before 1978, however, copyright duration is inextricably interdependent with the "formalities" of copyright notice, registration, and renewal. Without full compliance with these formalities, the copyright may have lapsed, and the work entered the public domain. This chapter will summarize and attempt to make practical sense of the law of copyright duration.

How long did the clock tick? The law before 1978 granted two sequential terms of copyright protection for publications. Proper use of a copyright notice gave an initial term of twenty-eight years. At the end of that term, the copyright owner was required to file a renewal application with the Copyright Office in order to receive the second and continuous term of protection.[11] Failure to file meant the copyright lapsed at the end of the first term. In the case of that 1940 publication, it could have entered the public domain on at least two occasions: in 1940 if published without notice, and in 1968 if not renewed.

Renewal of Copyrights

How long is the renewal term? The question does not have an easy answer. The renewal term was another twenty-eight years, but in the early 1960s the term was stretched to forty-seven years, for a total of seventy-five years of protection. In 1998, Congress added twenty more years to the protection for early works.[12] So today a work published before 1978 can generally have a total term of protection of ninety-five years.[13]

> Although early publications may generally have ninety-five years of protection, the rule actually reaches back only to 1923. Works published before 1923 were in the public domain when Congress extended the duration term by twenty years in 1998. Congress left those works outside the reach of copyright protection.

In 1992 Congress eliminated the renewal requirement for all existing copyrights.[14] Consider the simple example of a book published in 1970. The published copies needed to include a copyright notice to secure the initial twenty-eight years of protection. By the time the copyright was slated for renewal in 1998, Congress dropped the renewal requirement. The 1970 book received an automatic continuation of protection to the full ninety-five years available under today's law. By contrast, the book published in 1940 had to be renewed in 1968, otherwise the copyright expired at that time.

Foreign Works and Restoration

In general, the fundamental rules of American copyright law apply to domestic as well as to most foreign works that enter the jurisdictional boundaries of the United States. One essential rule of law: when in the United States, apply U.S. law. Pre-1978 law in the United States, with its formalities and fixed duration, was an international anomaly. For more than a century, nearly all countries had a system of automatic protection lasting for the life of the author plus at least fifty years.

The American system was therefore especially troublesome for foreign authors who had the benefit of automatic protection in their home country, but often did not know the compliance procedures of American law. Many works gained full protection in a foreign country, but went into the public domain inside U.S. boundaries. The United States faced diplomatic pressures to conform its law to international standards, and to remedy the perceived inequitable treatment that foreign works received under American law.

The eventual response was a complex twist of international law that "restored" copyright protection for many foreign works that had entered the public domain inside the United States for lack of formalities.[15] This outcome is yet another dose of confusion in the law. Many foreign and domestic publications from before 1978 entered the public domain for failure to comply with the formalities of notice and renewal. Domestic works remain in the public domain, while many foreign works were brought back under copyright protection.

> The "restoration" requirement was initially a limited provision adopted by Congress as part of the *North American Free Trade Agreement Act*, Public Law 103-182, *U.S. Statutes at Large* 107 (1993): 2057. Restoration later became more comprehensive under the agreement of the World Trade Organization. *Uruguay Round Agreements Act*, Public Law 103-465, *U.S. Statutes at Large* 108 (1994): 4809, 4976

> Which foreign countries have had their works "restored" under U.S. law? Almost all of them, starting with the 148 countries that are members of the World Trade Organization. For the latest listing, see http://www.wto.int.

The "restoration" became effective at the beginning of 1996. Copyrights gaining new life at that time continued through the end of the term they otherwise would have received.[16] For example, a Swiss publication from 1940 that was not renewed entered the public domain in the United States in 1968. In 1996 it once again became protected by copyright. Had the law not required formalities, American copyright law would have given ninety-five years of protection to the Swiss publication—until the year 2035. Therefore, once restored in 1996, the copyright continues to that same expiration in 2035.

> "Restoration" can apply to works that have entered the public domain for other reasons, too. For example, U.S. copyright did not apply to sound recordings until 1972. In 1996, foreign sound recordings from before 1972 were for the first time given copyright protection in the *Uruguay Round Agreements Act*, Public Law 103-465, *U.S. Statutes at Large* 108 (1994): 4809.

Practical Lessons for Users

What do these rules mean for the user of a pre-1978 work? An early work may well be in the public domain for failure to comply with formalities. To reach that conclusion, however, you may need to investigate the original publication of the work and whether a renewal appears in the records of the Copyright Office. Renewal records are public, and the Copyright Office will conduct searches for a fee. Online searches are also available through some database providers.

> Anytime you are tracking an owner or tracing a copyright, keep detailed records of your pursuit and findings. Your good-faith efforts to apply the law and track down facts can be important should anyone challenge your actions.

Even works that lacked the formality of renewal or notice may still be protected, if the work originated from one of the many foreign countries enjoying the benefits of the "restoration" provision. This twist applies to most, but not all, countries, and as usual the law includes many detailed nuances. A user of an early work clearly has a significant research project to complete before determining whether some publications really are in the public domain.

With respect to works created in or after 1978, users need to face the reality that the lack of a copyright notice or registration is not conclusive. Moreover, given the unusually long period of copyright protection for such newer works, the simple reality is that a user needs to assume that nearly all recent works are fully protected until learning otherwise from the author or publisher.

Important Lessons for Owners

Do not overlook the benefits of formalities for your new works. Placing the copyright notice on your work offers valuable information to readers who might need to locate you for permission or further information. The simple copyright notice can streamline searches for copyright owners and help assure that their interests will be respected. A proper copyright notice also has the legal effect of barring an infringer from claiming to be an "innocent infringer." This limited defense could apply if the user believed the activities were not infringing.[17]

Registering your work with the U.S. Copyright Office offers the practical benefit of creating a public pronouncement of your claim to the copyright, as well as an address for contacting you. Registration additionally grants important legal benefits in the unlikely event of a lawsuit.[18] These aspects of the law are covered in chapter 13, and they will in turn have some surprising and critical implications for librarians and educators who are struggling with "fair use" and thorny questions of infringement liability.

> To secure the full benefits of the registration, it usually must be completed before the alleged infringement occurred. *The simple lesson: register early!* For information about registration, visit the U.S. Copyright Office website: http://www.copyright.gov.

Notes

1. *U.S. Copyright Act*, 17 *U.S.C.* § 302 (2005).
2. For works created on or after January 1, 1978, copyright vests automatically at the time the work is "fixed." *U.S. Copyright Act*, 17 *U.S.C.* § 102 (2005).
3. *U.S. Copyright Act*, 17 *U.S.C.* § 102.
4. *Act of May 31, 1790*, ch. 15, sec. 1, *U.S. Statutes at Large* 1 (1790): 124 (repealed 1802).
5. The history of American copyright law is recounted in many articles and books, including Tyler T. Ochoa, "Patent and Copyright Term Extension and the Constitution: A Historical Perspective," *Journal of the Copyright Society of the U.S.A.* 49 (Fall 2001): 19–125; and Robert L. Bard and Lewis Kurlantzick, *Copyright Duration: Duration, Term Extension, the European Union and the Making of Copyright Policy* (San Francisco: Austin and Winfield, 1998).
6. *U.S. Copyright Act*, 17 *U.S.C.* §§ 405–406 (2005).
7. *U.S. Copyright Act*, 17 *U.S.C.* § 304 (2005).
8. *U.S. Copyright Act*, 17 *U.S.C.* § 302(a) (2005).
9. The same term applies to anonymous and pseudonymous works. *U.S. Copyright Act*, 17 *U.S.C.* § 302(c) (2005).
10. For specific legal benefits afforded by the law, see *U.S. Copyright Act*, 17 *U.S.C.* §§ 411–412 (2005).
11. *Act of March 4, 1909*, ch. 320, sec. 23–24, *U.S. Statutes at Large* 35 (1909): 1075, 1080.
12. *Sonny Bono Copyright Term Extension Act*, Public Law 105-298, *U.S. Statutes at Large* 112 (1998): 2827, codified in scattered sections of 17 *U.S.C.* (2005). See also *Eldred v. Ashcroft*, 537 U.S. 186 (2003).
13. *U.S. Copyright Act*, 17 *U.S.C.* § 304 (2005).
14. *Copyright Amendments Act of 1992*, Public Law 102-307, *U.S. Statutes at Large* 106 (1992): 264, 266, codified at 17 *U.S.C.* § 304 (2005).
15. *U.S. Copyright Act*, 17 *U.S.C.* § 104A (2005).
16. *U.S. Copyright Act*, 17 *U.S.C.* § 104A.
17. *U.S. Copyright Act*, 17 *U.S.C.* § 401(d) (2005).
18. See generally *U.S. Copyright Act*, 17 *U.S.C.* §§ 411–412 (2005).

4

Who Owns the Copyright?

KEY POINTS

- ■ The creator of a new work is the copyright owner.

- ■ Two or more authors working together may be "joint" copyright owners.

- ■ The copyright owner of a "work made for hire" is the employer.

- ■ Copyrights may be transferred by means of a written instrument signed by the copyright owner.

- ■ Institutional policies are important for clarifying or sharing rights to new works, but they must conform to legal requirements.

A vast range of works receive automatic copyright protection, and someone owns those legal rights. The general rule is that the owner of copyright is the person who does the creative work.[1] If you write the book, you own the copyright. If you take the photograph, you own the copyright. If you design the website, it is yours. The list goes on.

Yet some variations on this basic rule are of critical importance. First, two or more authors can own a single copyright "jointly." Second, someone might create a new work, but it may be a "work made for hire," and the copyright will belong to the employer. Finally, regardless of wherever the law might vest ownership, the copyright owner may transfer the copyright to a publisher or anyone else. Sorting and keeping track of ownership can be essential for managing copyrights and for tracing rights.

Joint Copyright Ownership

Many copyrights are the result of two or more authors working together. Two scientists may write a journal article. Three designers might work on a website over a period of months or years. An entering class of students might contribute to a mural in the school hall. These works may be "jointly" owned.

The Copyright Act defines a joint work as "a work prepared by two or more authors with the intention that their contributions be merged into inseparable or interdependent parts of a unitary whole."[2] "Inseparable" contributions might be blended into a coauthored textbook or article. "Interdependent" contributions might be the words and music for one song or the text and images for a multimedia work.

A joint work generally must meet two requirements. First, each coauthor must contribute copyrightable expression to the joint project. If one party gives only an idea for the project, that person has not provided copyrightable expression and therefore is not a joint author under the law.[3] Second, each contributor must have had the intent to create a joint work at the time the work was created. This "intent" refers to the authors' expectation that their contributions would be combined into a unified whole, not necessarily the specific requirement that the authors thought about ownership of their work in strictly legal terms.[4]

> Copyright protection for a jointly owned work usually lasts throughout the life of the last of the authors to die, plus seventy more years. *U.S. Copyright Act*, 17 *U.S.C.* § 302(b) (2005). Clever writers could involve youthful coauthors in order to boost the likelihood of prolonging legal rights. Keep in mind that if you are one of the joint owners, you may well outlive your coauthor and find yourself sharing legal rights with his or her children, grandchildren, or other heirs.

Problems with Joint Ownership

Joint ownership is astonishingly common. It is also a serious management headache. Each joint owner of a work holds an undivided share in the copyright.[5] Each co-owner can use or license the entire work as he or she wishes, but must account for profits to the other joint owners. On the other hand, each co-owner acting alone cannot transfer the copyright to another party or grant an exclusive right to use the work without the consent of the other co-owners.

Consider this simple example. You and a colleague jointly own the copyright to a research article. Each of you may individually post the paper to your websites. Each of you can permit other scholars and teachers to make and share copies of it. You can even collect a fee for giving permission, but you are liable to your co-owner for a share of the money. Acting alone, however, you cannot transfer the copyright to a publisher or anyone else, whether gratis or for payment. In fact, a joint owner acting alone cannot grant an exclusive license to use the work. For those transactions, all joint owners must participate together.[6]

Joint ownership easily gives rise to many management challenges. In many cases the best solution is a contract between authors, detailing a variety of concerns: who is able to make decisions about the use of the work; who is responsible for finances; who will be able to change or update the work; who can enter into publication agreements. Because one author will almost always outlive the other, joint owners should look ahead. They should plan for the management of their works, anticipating the time when children, grandchildren, and others inherit a share of the copyright.

Works Made for Hire

An important exception to the basic rule of copyright ownership is the doctrine of "work made for hire" (WMFH). For these works, the employer of the person who does the creative work is considered the author and the copyright owner.[7] The employer may be a firm, an organization, or an individual.

> In addition to affecting ownership, the WMFH doctrine changes the term of copyright protection. Ordinarily a work is protected for the life of the author plus 70 years. By contrast, a WMFH is protected for the shorter of either 95 years from first publication or 120 years from creation. Chapter 3 provides a detailed look at copyright duration.

Two basic situations can give rise to a work made for hire. The most common situation occurs when a work is prepared by an employee within the scope of his or her employment.[8] If the copyrighted work is created under these conditions, the work is deemed to be "for hire," and the copyright belongs from the outset to the employer.[9] No further agreement is required.

Examples of possible "works made for hire" created in an employment relationship are:

> Some of the examples and information about WMFH in this chapter also appear in one of the helpful publications from the U.S. Copyright Office. The Copyright Office issues a long list of "circulars" addressing many issues in the law in clear language. For the full list, see http://www.copyright.gov/circs/.

- A software program created by a staff programmer for Creative Computer Corporation
- A newspaper article written by a staff journalist for publication in a daily newspaper
- A musical arrangement written for XYZ Music Company by a salaried arranger on its staff

A second WMFH situation involves "independent contractors" (as opposed to employees). Here the statute becomes more exacting. The new work is "for hire" only if it is "specially ordered or commissioned" and is among the types of works itemized in the statute.[10] Even meeting those requirements is not enough for this version of WMFH; the parties must further expressly agree in a written instrument—signed by *both* parties—that the work shall be considered a WMFH. Only then will the new work be deemed "for hire" with all rights belonging to the hiring party.

> What works are listed in the WMFH statute? With respect to independent contractors, the statute can apply to works made "for use as a contribution to a collective work, as a part of a motion picture or other audiovisual work, as a translation, as a supplementary work, as a compilation, as an instructional text, as a test, as answer material for a test, or as an atlas."
>
> —*U.S. Copyright Act, 17 U.S.C. § 101 (2005)*

Who Is an Employee?

One of the most important and sometimes difficult issues surrounding the WMFH doctrine centers on whether the project was created by an "employee" or an "independent contractor." Common understandings of these terms may not necessarily be the law, and the result can have profound implications for copyright ownership. For example, you may pay a computer programmer a vast fortune to rework your business systems, or you may pay a tidy sum for photos of your children, but paying money does not make the work "for hire." The freelance programmer and the photography studio are most likely "independent contractors" and hold the copyrights—and get to keep the money.

> Newspaper articles are *not* on the list of eligible works in the WMFH statute, so how can they qualify as works made for hire? First, keep in mind that this list is relevant only in the case of independent contractors. Second, news articles may not be specified on the list, but the statute does encompass contributions to "collective" works. A news article can be a contribution to a newspaper, which is a "collective" work. The WMFH statute can consequently apply more broadly than might first appear.

A freelance contractor and an employee may work side by side on similar projects, only to have radically diverging ownership results. A newspaper may have staff reporters, and as employees, their articles are WMFH. A reporter at the next desk, however, may be an independent contractor. Her articles are WMFH only if they are on the list in the statute, and if she and the employer have entered into a written agreement that the articles will be regarded as "for hire."

Academic institutions and libraries often find themselves in a predicament with independent contractors. They pay thousands of dollars for the services of a photographer, a video producer, or a public relations firm to prepare publications, websites, and glossy brochures, only to discover later that the contractor retains the copyright and can control the use of the materials. The photographer can therefore ask for more money with each use of the pictures; the public relations firm can object when the images and words of a brochure are later restructured for the university website.

> The most important legal effect of a work's being "for hire" is a vesting of rights with the employer. In fact, the employer is legally defined to be the "author" of the new work, even though someone else actually did the creative work. Calling a work "for hire" has other important consequences. "Moral rights" cannot apply (see chapter 5), and a transfer of the copyright cannot be "terminated," as is sometimes allowed many decades after a transfer occurs.

The law offers at least one practical solution to this dilemma: copyrights may be transferred. If the law resolves that the photographer or programmer owns the copyright, but this is not the desired result, the parties may agree to move the ownership to the other party.

> Short of a transfer, the parties could enter into a license agreement that anticipates future needs and clarifies rights of use. Some contractors instinctively object to transferring copyrights. The parties may be satisfied with allowing the contractor to hold the copyrights, but agreeing to permit the hiring party to have specific rights to use the work. An "exclusive" license must be in writing and signed by the licensor. A "non-exclusive" license need not be in writing, but documenting the transaction is always a wise move.

Transfers of Copyright

Copyrights can be bought, sold, or simply given away. A transfer of the copyright or an exclusive grant or license to use the work is a transaction that must be in writing and must be signed by the copyright owner making the transfer.[11] Let's assume you write a song or create a painting and hold the copyright. You could give away or sell the copyright to these works, but the transfer is legally valid only if the terms of the transfer are in writing and are signed by you.

Transferring the object itself is distinct from transferring the copyright. For example, you may create a painting and sell it to an appreciative collector at a hefty price. But selling the painting does not include a sale of the copyright, unless you specifically document the copyright transfer in a signed writing. Neither a high price nor an oral statement of transfer will substitute for the statutory requirements. We actually experience this rule on a daily basis. We go to the bookstore and buy a book. We have purchased the book, but we have not acquired the copyright.

> The Stanford Law School serves as home to an exciting new project called Creative Commons, at http://creativecommons.org. Users are free to mold a license that allows others who find their content on the Internet to use it under the conditions the copyright owner has specified in the license.

In the academic world, we also routinely transfer our copyrights. A professor writes an article and, as the author, likely owns the copyright. Some journal publishers, however, upon accepting the article for publication, require that the author transfer the copyright to the publisher as one of the terms of the written and signed publication agreement. But not all journal publishers require assignment of the copyright. Whether the author or the publisher owns the copyright to a particular article is a factual matter that needs to be investigated with each work.

> Authors who are faced with a publication contract that seeks transfer of the copyright should not hesitate to negotiate new terms or at least reserve rights to use their own work in future teaching and writing, or they should find a different publisher. Project RoMEO offers a wealth of information and alternative language for publication agreements. See http://www.lboro.ac.uk/departments/ls/disresearch/romeo/.

Institutional Policies

These rules of copyright ownership, notably the rules of WMFH, do not always apply clearly and neatly. Sometimes, to resolve doubts and lingering questions, an author and an employer may need a contract specifying the allocation of rights to use the work and the distribution of royalties or income. Many academic institutions develop formal policies in an effort to specify whether new works belong to the institution or to the author.

The custom at most colleges and universities is to leave most copyrights with faculty authors, and this tradition may not change drastically in the near future. Yet, careful and meticulous rethinking of institutional policies is gaining pace. Some policymakers are reckoning with the changing nature of academic work and are pursuing policies that shift to the institution some ownership rights in faculty works. The growth of distance education and the considerable financial consequences of creating and marketing new works have stirred the need to reexamine the feasibility of traditional and simplistic concepts of intellectual property at educational institutions.

Moreover, recent court rulings have drawn into question the tradition of faculty ownership of copyright and the effectiveness of institutional policies. These courts have found that many works created at colleges and universities are in fact "for hire," vesting the copyright with the employer. The courts have also concluded that general policy statements may be insufficient to effect a transfer of the copyright to the employee. The Copyright Act specifies that a WMFH belongs to the employer "unless the parties have expressly agreed otherwise in a written instrument signed by them."[12] A general policy, however, is ordinarily not signed by the parties to each individual transfer of rights.

> "The Policy is patently inadequate to overcome the presumption of Brown's ownership under the work made for hire doctrine."
>
> —District Judge William E. Smith
> in *Foraste v. Brown University*

An international initiative encouraging innovative policymaking at universities is the Zwolle Group, based in the Netherlands. For more information, see http://www.surf.nl/copyright/.

Recent Cases and New Possibilities

A few recent cases have raised new questions about WMFH in higher education and have drawn new attention to the importance of effective and creative policies. Consider the following cases:

> *Forasté v. Brown University*, 248 F. Supp. 2d 71 (D.R.I. 2003). The court in Rhode Island held that photographs taken by a university employee belonged to the university as a WMFH. The university policy that purported to grant copyrights to employees was insufficient to meet the statutory requirements for a transfer.[13]

> *Vanderhurst v. Colorado Mountain College Dist.*, 16 F. Supp. 2d 1297 (D. Colo. 1998). A professor developed teaching materials for instruction at the college, but disputed their ownership after leaving his faculty position. The Colorado court ruled that a professor's instructional materials were WMFH and belonged to the college.[14]

These cases do not necessarily undermine the value of universities' copyright policies. Instead, they make clear that such policies must be developed and implemented in strict accord with the law—perhaps paired with detailed, written agreements that faculty and university officials will need to sign individually. Most of all, the cases emphasize the critical importance of having a policy in order to shape the outcome of ownership questions, rather than relying solely on the defaults of the law.

The concept of "unbundling" the rights of copyright ownership has its roots in a project involving the present author for the California State University (CSU). The outcome was a pamphlet titled *Ownership of New Works at the University: Unbundling of Rights and the Pursuit of Higher Learning* (1997). Portions of this document were revised in 2003 and became part of a position paper from the CSU that is available at http://www.calstate.edu/AcadSen/Records/Reports/Intellectual_Prop_Final.pdf.

Thoughtful policies and agreements also offer the opportunity to share or "unbundle" the rights that would normally vest with a single copyright owner. Placing all rights with either the individual author or the employer can give rise to conflicts between the parties. Instead, agreements that detail allocation of rights among the parties may allow a work to be used by the author and the institution simultaneously, effectively, and equitably. Policymakers are now often looking beyond simple formulas to find more creative and desirable solutions to the challenges of copyright ownership.

Notes

1. "Copyright in a work protected under this title vests initially in the author or authors of the work." *U.S. Copyright Act*, 17 U.S.C. § 201 (2005).
2. *U.S. Copyright Act*, 17 U.S.C. § 101 (2005).
3. *Gaiman v. McFarlane*, 360 F.3d 644 (7th Cir. 2004).

4. *Erickson v. Trinity Theatre, Inc.*, 202 F.3d 1227 (7th Cir. 1994).

5. *U.S. Copyright Act*, 17 *U.S.C.* § 201(a) (2005).

6. *U.S. Copyright Act*, 17 *U.S.C.* § 204(a) (2005).

7. *U.S. Copyright Act*, 17 *U.S.C.* § 201(b) (2005).

8. For examples of how courts interpret "scope of employment" under the work-made-for-hire doctrine, see *Avtec Systems, Inc. v. Peiffer*, 21 F.3d 568 (4th Cir. 1994); *Community for Creative Non-Violence v. Reid*, 490 U.S. 730 (1989).

9. *U.S. Copyright Act*, 17 *U.S.C.* § 201(b) (2005).

10. See the definition of "work made for hire" at *U.S. Copyright Act*, 17 *U.S.C.* § 101 (2005).

11. *U.S. Copyright Act*, 17 *U.S.C.* § 204 (2005).

12. *U.S. Copyright Act*, 17 *U.S.C.* § 201(b).

13. Another recent case reached essentially the same conclusion based on remarkably similar facts. *Manning v. Parkland College*, 109 F. Supp. 2d 976 (C.D. Ill. 2000).

14. The same Colorado court, in an unrelated case, ruled that a professor's research article could also be a WMFH. *University of Colorado Foundation, Inc. v. American Cyanamid*, 880 F. Supp. 1387 (D. Colo. 1995).

5

The Rights of Copyright Owners

KEY POINTS

■ Copyright owners have exclusive rights to:

    Reproduce the work

    Distribute the work

    Prepare derivative works

    Publicly display the work

    Publicly perform the work

■ Some "works of visual art" also have moral rights.

■ Congress has responded to technological change by granting additional rights with respect to some works.

The owner of the copyright to a specific work has certain "exclusive rights" with respect to the work. In this context, "exclusive" means that the copyright owner may exercise those rights and other individuals may not—unless authorized by the owner. For example, owners hold the right to make copies of the work. If someone else makes an unauthorized copy, it may be an infringement. Section 106 of the Copyright Act itemizes the central rights of a copyright owner:[1]

■ The right to reproduce the work in copies

■ The right to distribute the work publicly

■ The right to make derivative works

■ The right to display the work publicly

■ The right to perform the work publicly

The rights of owners are fundamental to the concept of copyright law. By defining these rights, the law is also defining the range of possible infringements. You can violate the law only by infringing rights held by the owner. A copyright owner does not control all activities with respect to the work—only those activities specifically encompassed by the law.

This chapter will demonstrate that the rights of owners are hardly static. Congress has revised the statutes through the years, steadily expanding owners' rights, most recently in 1998. In the meantime, courts have regularly redefined and applied the law for new situations and needs.

> The first U.S. copyright statute, in 1790, granted only rights to make copies of works. Congress added performance rights in 1831, permitting musicians and playwrights to control live performances and not merely sales of copies of their works. The act of 1909 expanded basic rights to something similar to the current list.

Reproduction and Distribution Rights

The right of reproduction of a work means just what it says. Reproducing a work can occur in many circumstances and by means of a vast range of technological tools. We reproduce works when we photocopy pages from a text, when we quote a sentence into a new article, and even when we take verbatim notes from research materials. We reproduce works when we make a transparency of a cartoon to show in class, when we make a videotape that captures images of paintings on the wall, and when we digitize images for our websites or multimedia works. We reproduce works when we print a page or download an MP3 from the Internet.

> A case of considerable importance concluded that one makes a copy of computer software when it is loaded into the random-access memory (RAM) of a computer.
>
> —*MAI Systems Corp. v. Peak Computer, Inc.*, 991 F.2d 511 (9th Cir. 1993)

The distribution of works is also surprisingly common. We raise the possibility of distributing copyrighted works when we hand out photocopies in class, make documents available on our website, send e-mail attachments, or even allow people to borrow books from our personal or library collections. A bookstore's survival depends on successful distribution—through sales—of copyrighted works to its customers.

This right extends only to distributions made "to the public." Privately lending a book to a friend is not "to the public," but a library open for general use, or a store looking for maximum sales, is most certainly distribution to the public.

Derivative Works

Of all the rights of the copyright owner, the right to make derivative works may be the most difficult to explain, yet examples are also common. A "derivative work" is a work based upon one or more preexisting works.[2] A common example of a derivative work is a motion picture made from a novel. An author writes the novel and owns the copyright to it. The motion picture studio needs to secure permission from the novelist before preparing a screenplay and shooting the film. Derivatives can be as simple as the toy in a McDonald's Happy Meal that is based on a Disney movie character.

> A digital version of a photograph showing a cityscape, significantly altered, is a derivative work.
>
> —*Tiffany Design, Inc. v. Reno-Tahoe Specialty, Inc.*, 55 F. Supp. 2d 1113 (D. Nev. 1999)

Scholarly works rarely generate lucrative movie deals. Nevertheless, the routine activities of academics and librarians often involve derivative works. Some examples include a digitized version of an analog recording, image, or text; a teacher's manual and other works to support a textbook; artwork from or inspired by an existing picture or image; and the production of a new ballet or play from an existing story.

The range of possible derivative works is extensive:

- An index to a book
- A sound recording of a musical composition
- An abridgement of a novel
- A translation

Derivative works sometimes create conundrums. Consider a simple example. Ancient Greek poems may have no legal protection in their original version, but a new translation is a derivative. The translation, however, is an "original" work entitled to independent copyright protection. Thus, a movie based on the translation is a derivative of that copyrighted work; permission from the translator is in order. But if the filmmaker turns instead to the original (which is presumably in the public domain), the movie may still be a derivative, but not a violation of either the original or the translation.

Whether the movie is a derivative of the original or is a derivative of a derivative (i.e., the translation), the filmmaker can have copyright protection for the new movie. But be careful. A derivative work made without permission of the owner of the original work (if still under copyright) can be an infringement and may be denied legal protection. The lesson is fairly simple. Be sure to check with the copyright owner before investing time and energy to make a derivative work.

Public Performance and Display

Performances and displays are common occurrences in higher education. A "display" can be the simple showing of a page of text or a picture. A work can be "performed" in many ways: when text is read aloud; when lines of a play are recited or acted; when a videotape or a film is shown on a screen or monitor; or when a song is played or sung aloud. The performance or display can become a possible infringement only when it is "public."[3] A "public" performance or display occurs, among other circumstances, when it is made to a substantial number of persons beyond the usual circle of friends, family, and social acquaintances.[4]

> Not all rights apply to all types of works. Only in 1995 did Congress extend the "performance" right to sound recordings, but only when made "by means of a digital audio transmission." *Digital Performance Right in Sound Recordings Act of 1995*, Public Law 104-39, *U.S. Statutes at Large* 109 (1995): 336. This development is examined later in this chapter.

We frequently make public displays and performances of copyrighted works. Up and down the halls of libraries, schools, and museums one can find scores of pictures, essays, and books out for public viewing. Why are schools not liable for pinning student essays on the bulletin boards or for hanging pictures on the walls? Why are libraries not liable for placing their collections in public view? Why are museums still in business?

The answer to these questions lies in the exceptions to the rights of owners. Understanding the rights of owners requires an appreciation that the law establishes rights, but then tempers them with exceptions or "limitations" that are detailed later in this book. The U.S. Copyright Act includes several important exceptions to the performance and display rights of the copyright owner. Most saliently, a specific exception to the display right of the copyright owner allows the owner of an original work or a lawfully made copy of the work, such as a painting, a poster, or a photograph, to display that work where it is physically located. Thus, the museum can hang art on the walls, teachers can put posters in the classroom, the library can place books in display cases, and you can project slides onto a screen.[5]

No similarly broad exception, however, applies to performances. Consequently, no statutory exception covers the prospect of showing a movie in an auditorium or acting out a play on a school stage. On the other hand, a more specific provision of the law permits displays and performances in the context of "face-to-face" classroom instruction.[6] Therefore, teachers and students in the traditional classroom setting may read text, recite poetry, play videos, sing songs, and even show full sets of art slides.

> The generous provision for performances and displays of copyrighted works in the classroom does not apply to distance learning. The TEACH Act restructured the law in 2002 and is examined in detail in chapter 11. A roster of various other exceptions is surveyed in chapter 6.

Moral Rights

A relatively recent addition to owners' rights in the United States is the concept of "moral rights." Moral rights apply only to a narrow class of works.[7] In 1990 Congress amended the Copyright Act by granting "moral rights" with respect to certain "works of visual art."[8] Moral rights in general apply only to original works of art, sculpture, and other works of visual art that are produced in 200 copies or fewer.[9] For example, moral rights may apply to a limited-series lithograph, but likely do not apply to a photograph used in a mass-market magazine.

Moral rights grant to an artist the right to have his or her name kept on the work or to have the artist's name removed from it if the work has been altered in a way objectionable to the artist. Moral rights also give artists limited abilities to prevent their works from being defaced or destroyed.[10]

> Moral rights in the United States apply narrowly and only to some works of art. The concept applies much more broadly under the laws of many other countries. The protection of moral rights is required under the Berne Convention, and the United States adopted the concept with considerable reluctance.

A leading case on the issue of moral rights awarded monetary damages to an artist whose work was intentionally destroyed. The federal district court ruled that the city of Indianapolis violated the moral rights of a sculptor when the city demolished his large, metal work that had been installed on city property.[11]

Digital Audio Transmissions

Music receives peculiar treatment under the U.S. Copyright Act in many respects—including distinctly different rights of public performance. Compositions, or "musical works," long have received copyright protection and the benefit of all fundamental rights. However, sound recordings first gained federal copyright protection only in 1972.[12]

Congress at that time granted rights of reproduction and distribution to sound recordings, but not public performance rights. When a radio station played a new song on the air, therefore, the composer had a performance right and received a royalty. By contrast, the owner of the separate copyright to the recording had no performance rights and was not entitled to any payment. That owner could receive money from sales of recordings, because the copyright in the sound recording included rights of reproduction and distribution.

The development of the Internet as a medium for delivering music has threatened sales of CDs and other copies of recordings. If a user can receive transmitted performances of selected recordings on demand, the user has little need to buy CDs.[13] To protect the interests of copyright owners of the recordings, Congress in 1995 granted performance rights to them, but only in the context of "digital audio performances."[14] The statute is enormously complex and runs for pages of convoluted conditions and exceptions.[15] In general, an "interactive" digital system—including a website—that transmits recordings on demand may now implicate the performance rights of both the composer and the performer.

Digital Millennium Copyright Act

The Digital Millennium Copyright Act (DMCA) added two new rights to the arsenal of copyright owners. The law now prohibits the "circumvention" of technological protection systems. That is, if you crack the protective code on a disk or bypass the password interface to access data, you may have violated this new right. The DMCA also barred the removal of "copyright management information" from a copyrighted work. Under some conditions, removing the author's name or stripping away technological conditions for using materials may amount to a new form of copyright violation.

These new provisions added by the DMCA have proven to be more complicated than expected, and they have been used to constrain activity in some most unlikely ways. The DMCA receives a more detailed examination in chapter 15.

Notes

1. *U.S. Copyright Act*, 17 *U.S.C.* § 106 (2005).
2. The statute defines a derivative work as "a work based upon one or more preexisting works, such as a translation, musical arrangement, dramatization, fictionalization, motion picture version, sound recording, art reproduction, abridgment, condensation, or any other form in which a work may be recast, transformed, or adapted." *U.S. Copyright Act*, 17 *U.S.C.* § 101 (2005).
3. *U.S. Copyright Act*, 17 *U.S.C.* §§ 106(4), 106(5) (2005).
4. *U.S. Copyright Act*, 17 *U.S.C.* § 101.
5. *U.S. Copyright Act*, 17 *U.S.C.* § 109(c) (2005).
6. *U.S. Copyright Act*, 17 *U.S.C.* § 110(1) (2005).
7. Moral rights are provided to a "work of visual art." A "work of visual art" is narrowly defined under the statute. See *U.S. Copyright Act*, 17 *U.S.C.* §§ 101, 106A (2005).
8. *Visual Artists Rights Act of 1990*, Public Law 101-650, *U.S. Statutes at Large* 104 (1990): 5089, 5128–5133, codified at *U.S. Copyright Act*, 17 *U.S.C.* §§ 101, 106A (2005).
9. *U.S. Copyright Act*, 17 *U.S.C.* § 101.
10. *U.S. Copyright Act*, 17 *U.S.C.* § 106A (2005).
11. *Martin v. Indianapolis*, 982 F. Supp. 625 (S.D. Ind. 1997), *aff'd*, 192 F.3d 608 (7th Cir. 1999).
12. *Act of October 15, 1971*, Public Law 92-140, *U.S. Statutes at Large* 85 (1971): 391.
13. See *A&M Records, Inc. v. Napster, Inc.*, 239 F.3d 1004 (9th Cir. 2001).
14. *Digital Performance Right in Sound Recordings Act of 1995*, Public Law 104-39, *U.S. Statutes at Large* 109 (1995): 336.
15. *U.S. Copyright Act*, 17 *U.S.C.* § 114(d) (2005).

6

Exceptions to the Rights of Owners

KEY POINTS

- Fair use is the most important and best known of the exceptions to the rights of owners.

- The Copyright Act includes numerous exceptions to owners' rights.

- Many exceptions are vital to education and librarianship.

- Congress continues to enact new exceptions, creating new opportunities to use copyrighted works.

One of the most important aspects of copyright ownership is that the rights of owners are not complete. The law grants a broad set of rights to a broad range of materials, then proceeds to carve out exceptions to those rights. The U.S. Copyright Act includes no fewer than sixteen statutory provisions that establish exceptions to the rights of the copyright owner. The broadest and best known of these exceptions is "fair use." Most of the other statutory exceptions are relevant only to certain industries and require careful legal guidance to comprehend and apply. Some exceptions apply only to the needs of the music, cable television, and other commercial industries. These statutes can stretch over many pages of convoluted text.

A few of the statutory exceptions apply specifically to the needs of educators and librarians. The language of these provisions is also relatively clear and direct—at least in comparison to other acts of Congress. One statutory exception allows libraries to make copies of materials for research or preservation; another exception allows performances and displays of works in the classroom and in distance education.

Few of these statutory provisions are as generous as one might hope. The statutes may allow uses that would otherwise be infringements, but most of the exceptions apply only to specifically identified types of works, only under detailed circumstances, and only for the prescribed purposes. By contrast, fair use is unusual in its breadth and flexibility.

The following is a summary of exceptions that are of greatest importance to educators and librarians. The section numbers indicate where they are codified in the U.S. Copyright Act. Later chapters offer a closer look at many of these provisions.

Section 107: Fair use. This provision may be thought of as the "umbrella" exception. It is broad and flexible in its scope, and it can apply to a potentially unlimited variety of unpredictable situations where someone uses copyrighted works, ranging from simple quotations to complex cutting and pasting of pieces of works into a new collage, multimedia work, or website.[1] Fair use is also an "umbrella" in another sense. It is the exception that one looks to for protection when the other statutes do not apply. For example, if your library is seeking to make copies, but your plans do not fit the required conditions of the next statute, Section 108, you can look to fair use as a possible alternative.

> Fair use is the subject of more detailed examination in chapters 7, 8, and 9. Fair use is much debated and maligned, but it is crucial for the daily success of our teaching, learning, and research.

Section 108: Library copying. Unlike the flexibility and general nature of fair use, this statute is more detailed in its application. Section 108 provides that most academic and public libraries, as well as many other libraries, may make copies of certain types of works for specific purposes. Section 108 permits preservation copying, copying of individual works for research and study, and copying for interlibrary loans.[2] Chapter 12 examines this statute in detail and shows that its benefits do not always apply to all copies of all types of works.

> The Digital Millennium Copyright Act of 1998 amended Section 108 to clarify when libraries may use digital technology to preserve works in the collection and to reproduce works when their technological format has become obsolete. This point and all of Section 108 are detailed in chapter 12.

Section 109(a): The first-sale doctrine. This important exception limits the "distribution rights" of the copyright holder by providing that once the owner authorizes the release of lawfully made copies of a work, those copies may in turn be passed along to others by sale, rental, loan, gift, or other transfer.[3] Without this important exception, a bookstore could not sell you a book, the library could not let you check out a book, the video store could not rent a movie, you could not sell your used DVDs on eBay, and you could not give books, CDs, and videos to your friends as birthday presents. Without this exception, all of those transactions might be unlawful distributions of someone else's copyrighted works. You can begin to see that the exceptions may be necessary to make daily activities feasible.

Section 109(c): Exception for public displays. This provision greatly limits the "public display right" of the copyright owner by allowing the owner of an original or a lawfully made copy of a work to display it to the public at the place where the work is located.[4] Thus, the art museum that owns a painting may hang it on the wall and let the public enter the front door to view it. The bookstore can place books on display in front windows, and the library may put its rare and valuable works in display cases for all to see. Without this exception, those activities could be infringements. This exception is so extraordinarily broad that it effectively limits the copyright owner's display right to situations where the image is transmitted by television or by other systems to a location beyond where the copyrighted work itself is actually located.

Section 110(1): Displays and performances in face-to-face teaching. This exception is crucial for the functioning and survival of basic teaching methods. It sweepingly allows performances and displays of all types of works in the setting of a classroom or similar place at most educational institu-

Section 110(1) is generous in its application for classroom uses, but always keep in mind that it only permits "displays and performances." It does not authorize making copies of materials, even in the classroom setting. This statute, and the following provision for distance education, are examined in detail in chapter 11.

tions, from preschool to graduate school. It allows instructors and students to recite poetry, read plays, show videos, play music, project slides, and engage in many other performances and displays of protected works in the classroom setting. This exception benefits multitudes of educators and students every day. Its rather simple language includes few restrictions or burdensome conditions.

Section 110(2): Displays and performances in distance learning.

Once we turn on the cameras or upload instruction onto websites—transmitting the classroom experience through distance learning—the law makes an abrupt shift. Section 110(2) was fully revised in 2002 with passage of the TEACH Act.[5] While the new law offers many new opportunities, it is also replete with restrictions and conditions. The ability to make displays and performances in distance education is remarkably more constrained than the allowed uses in the classroom. For more detailed information about the TEACH Act, see chapter 11.

Section 117: Computer software.

This provision generally allows the owner of a copy of a computer program to modify the program to work on his or her computer or computer platform, and to make a backup copy of the software to use in the event of damage to or destruction of the original copy.[6] For most computer users, the ability to load copies of software is usually addressed in the license accompanying the program, minimizing the need to rely on the statute for that right.

The Digital Millennium Copyright Act amended Section 117 to clarify that computer software may be reproduced in order to repair the computer on which the program was originally loaded.

Section 120: Architectural works.

Architectural designs are protected by copyright, giving architects the right to protect their designs from copying and from construction without permission. But Section 120 makes clear that once a building is constructed at a place visible to the public, anyone may make a picture of that building without infringing the copyright in the architectural design. Architectural historians and structural engineers can be spared from infringement when they take pictures of existing structures and use them in teaching and research, or for almost any other purpose. Moreover, the photograph itself is a new copyrighted work apart from the copyright in the architectural design.

Section 121: Special formats for persons who are blind or have other disabilities.

Congress added this provision in 1996 to allow certain types of organizations to make specific types of formats of published, nondramatic literary works so that they may be useful to persons who are blind or have other disabilities. Educational institutions and libraries may be able to take advantage of this provision by making large-print or Braille versions of some works in their collections. Like so many statutory exceptions in the Copyright Act, this law grants rights only to certain qualified organizations and applies only to a defined class of works.

Section 110(8) is yet another exception for the benefit of blind persons. It allows a performance of a nondramatic literary work to be transmitted by a special transmission device directed to blind or other handicapped persons, if the transmission is made through a governmental body, a noncommercial educational broadcast station, or an authorized radio subcarrier.

—*U.S. Copyright Act*, 17 U.S.C. § 110(8) (2005)

The U.S. Copyright Act includes many other statutory exceptions. Some are brief, such as a grant to horticulture organizations to perform musical works.[7] Some run for pages of convoluted text, such as the relentlessly technical statute allowing the rebroadcast of cable television programs.[8] A brief summary can hardly reflect the parameters of each law.

What happens if you simply cannot meet all of the requirements for applying one of the exceptions? You still have choices. You can seek permission. You can rearrange your plans in order to fit within the statute. You can find alternative materials that may not be protected by copyright. You may also turn once again to fair use. At the beginning of this chapter, fair use was described as an "umbrella." Fair use can reach broadly to many uses and many activities that the other more specific statutes may never have contemplated. Fair use can apply to all types of works and have meaning in situations and with technologies that Congress may never have anticipated. These are among the greatest virtues of fair use. Its flexibility gives fair use value when other exceptions fall short. The next four chapters offer a careful and pragmatic understanding of the law of fair use.

> Permission may come from the author, publisher, or other party that holds the rights to the work you want to use. You may secure permission directly from the rights holder, or through a licensing agent, such as the Copyright Clearance Center. More information about these possibilities appears in chapter 17 of this book.

Notes

1. See *NXIVM Corp. v. Ross Institute*, 364 F.3d 471 (2d Cir. 2004).
2. *U.S. Copyright Act*, 17 *U.S.C.* § 108 (2005).
3. *U.S. Copyright Act*, 17 *U.S.C.* § 109(a) (2005).
4. *U.S. Copyright Act*, 17 *U.S.C.* § 109(c) (2005).
5. *Technology, Education, and Copyright Harmonization Act of 2002*, Public Law 107-273, *U.S. Statutes at Large* 116 (2002): 1910, codified at 17 *U.S.C.* § 110(2) (2005).
6. *U.S. Copyright Act*, 17 *U.S.C.* § 117 (2005).
7. *U.S. Copyright Act*, 17 *U.S.C.* § 110(6) (2005).
8. *U.S. Copyright Act*, 17 *U.S.C.* § 111 (2005).

7 Fair Use: Getting Started

KEY POINTS

- ▇ Fair use is vital to the growth of knowledge.

- ▇ Fair use is based on a balancing of four factors set forth in the statute.

- ▇ Fair use can apply to a full range of materials and activities.

- ▇ Fair use has no definite boundaries.

Fair use has many descriptions and definitions. It can be defined as a limited right to use copyrighted works—normally under confined circumstances—especially for purposes that have social benefits. The statute itself indicates that fair use typically applies to activities such as education, research, news reporting, criticism, and commentary. By fostering these pursuits, the law of fair use can be important for advancing knowledge and communicating ideas. Yet fair use does not allow everything. This chapter offers insights into the meaning and the limits of fair use.

Fair use is both an extraordinary opportunity and a source of constant confusion. Fair use has been the target of steady challenge, and it is the object of enormous praise. Fair use is, for education and research, the most important of the many exceptions to the rights of copyright owners. It is flexible and adaptable to the many unpredictable situations and needs that occur as we pursue diverse projects and apply innovative technologies. Fair use can possess meaning for all types of media and all types of works. The most extraordinary difficulty of fair use, however, is that it often has a new scope and meaning for each set of circumstances.

Fair use can be a bit of a bother, but understanding and applying the law can be vital for the growth of knowledge. Fair use is an essential balance to the widening range of rights that copyright law grants to owners. At various times, fair use has been called a "right" and a "privilege," but whatever the label, the doctrine is a legally sanctioned opportunity. It allows the public to make limited uses of copyrighted works—uses that might otherwise be infringement—especially for advancing knowledge or to serve some other important social objective.

Fair use can rescue many would-be infringements and turn them into lawful uses, but only within limits. Consider some of the most common uses of copyrighted works. A short quotation from an existing paper into a new report could constitute an unlawful "reproduction" of the quoted portions of the work. Hitting the print key for a paper copy of a web page can also be a reproduction. When a TV news crew broadcasts a downtown festival, the program may include images of outdoor art and clips of music in the background. The broadcast could be a "public performance" or "public display" or other infringement of the art or music. The right of fair use may well rescue many of these activities from legal perdition.

While the flexibility of fair use is one of its greatest strengths, it is also the source of uncertainty. Reasonable people disagree on what is "fair," and no one has a definitive, legally binding "answer" to most fair-use questions. Congress deliberately created a flexible fair-use statute that gives no exact parameters.[1] Fair use depends on the circumstances of each case.[2]

Section 107 of the U.S. Copyright Act sets forth the fundamental law of fair use, and it articulates four factors to evaluate and to balance in the analysis:[3]

- The purpose of the use, including a nonprofit educational purpose
- The nature of the copyrighted work
- The amount of the work used
- The effect of the use on the potential market for, or value of, the original work

These concepts are rooted in a series of judicial rulings stretching back to 1841.[4] Courts examined and refined the doctrine of fair use for more than a century until, in 1976, Congress for the first time enacted a statute securing an explicit place for fair use in the larger equation of American copyright law.[5]

> The case of *Folsom v. Marsh* is commonly cited as the wellspring of American fair use. In his elaborate opinion from 1841, Justice Joseph Story isolated variables that impinge on the determination of fair use, and those variables are remarkably similar to the four factors of the current law.

In applying the statutory factors, most of us might agree that short quotations from published works in a scholarly publication are fair use. On the other hand, the greater the excerpt quoted, for example, the less likely it will be "fair." These examples are relatively easy to grasp, but difficult questions surround more complex challenges involving innovative uses of distinctive materials, such as standardized survey instruments, videotapes, or computer software. In recent years, courts have ruled on fair use as applied to rap versions of pop songs, thumbnail images of photographs on the Internet, and contorted Barbie dolls in modern art.[6]

> In *Higgins v. Detroit Educational Broadcasting Foundation*, 4 F. Supp. 2d 701 (E.D. Mich. 1998), the court allowed as fair use the incorporation of short excerpts of a musical work into the background of a production that was broadcast on a local PBS affiliate and sold in limited copies to educational institutions.

Possible "fair use" examples are innumerable. Although fair use can apply to a vast range of situations yet to be imagined, not all uses will be "fair." Moreover, each new situation requires fresh application of the four factors, and—short of an authoritative court ruling—the analysis may never produce easy or absolute answers. For librarians and educators, the state of the law can be even more frustrating. Through nearly two centuries of fair-use jurisprudence, courts have provided little direct guidance about fair use in the library or educational setting. The fair use of materials in scholarly endeavors is rarely the subject of judicial decisions, due probably to high litigation costs and attorney fees. Yet courts are not insensitive to academic needs, and the fair-use statute acknowledges explicitly the importance of educational needs. The next two chapters of this book examine the court rulings of particular importance to education and librarianship.

> Fair use has an important connection to the registration of copyrighted works. Recall from chapter 3 that registration of a work with the U.S. Copyright Office is not required for copyright protection. Chapter 13, nevertheless, explains how timely registration can allow an owner to obtain greater damages against an infringer. However, educators and librarians can have the benefit of eliminating the additional liabilities if they understand and apply fair use in a good-faith manner.

The Fair-Use Statute

Fair use is the subject of numerous misconceptions and myths. The best place to obtain a clear understanding of fair use is the statute itself—the real source of fair-use law in the United States. You might be surprised to learn that the fair-use statute takes hardly a minute to read and is remarkably simple and clear by comparison to many other federal statutes:

> Notwithstanding the provisions of sections 106 and 106A, the fair use of a copyrighted work, including such use by reproduction in copies or phonorecords or by any other means specified by that section, for purposes such as criticism, comment, news reporting, teaching (including multiple copies for classroom use), scholarship, or research, is not an infringement of copyright. In determining whether the use made of a work in any particular case is a fair use the factors to be considered shall include—
>
> (1) the purpose and character of the use, including whether such use is of a commercial nature or is for nonprofit educational purposes;
>
> (2) the nature of the copyrighted work;
>
> (3) the amount and substantiality of the portion used in relation to the copyrighted work as a whole; and
>
> (4) the effect of the use upon the potential market for or value of the copyrighted work.
>
> The fact that a work is unpublished shall not itself bar a finding of fair use if such finding is made upon consideration of all the above factors.

That is it. That is the statute on fair use. The statute establishes the framework for answering the extensive variety of questions you might have about clipping materials for websites, quoting from articles, making handouts for teaching, or sampling other music in a rap-music recording. Numerous court cases apply that framework to the facts at issue in order to determine whether an activity is fair use or infringement.

> The full text of the entire U.S. Copyright Act is available from many sources. The U.S. Copyright Office seeks to keep the full text, updated with all amendments, available on its website at http://www.copyright.gov/title17/.

A Closer Look at the Statute

Of course, the law is never so simple. Fair use is the subject of numerous books, thousands of articles, and a growing cascade of court opinions. The following chapters offer detailed insights, but for now, figure 7.1 offers a closer look at the language of the statute itself. Understanding fair use in any particular setting best begins with an overview of the language from Congress. The words of the statute may be relatively simple, but they are rich with meaning.

FIGURE 7.1 *Decoding the Language of Fair Use*

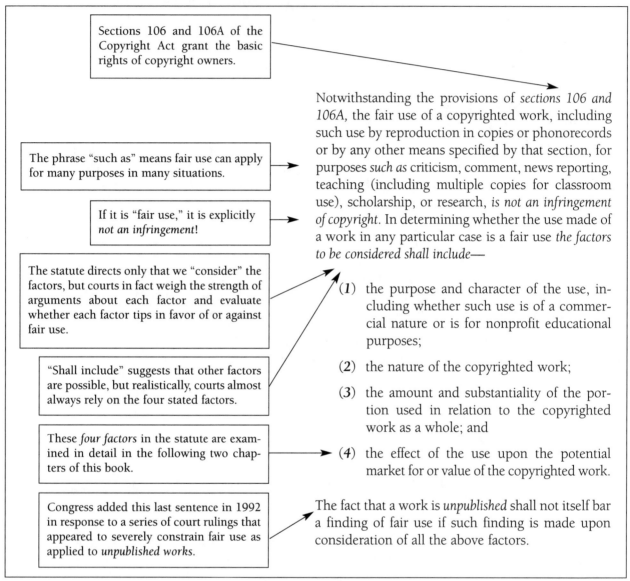

Kenneth D. Crews, *Copyright Law for Librarians and Educators* (ALA Editions, 2006)

Principles for Working with Fair Use

The following chapters tell more about the meaning of fair use, but always keep in mind the following practical principles for working with this important copyright doctrine.

Fair use is a balancing test. You need to evaluate and apply the four factors, but you do not need to satisfy all of them.[7] The pivotal question is whether the factors overall lean in favor of or against fair use.

Fair use is highly fact-sensitive. The meaning and application of the factors will depend on the specific facts of each situation. If you change the facts, you need to evaluate the factors anew.

Don't reach hasty conclusions. The question of fair use requires evaluation of all four factors. Do not conclude that you are within fair use merely because your use is for nonprofit education.[8] Similarly, a commercial use can also be within fair use after examining all factors.[9]

> Chapter 6 summarizes some of the other statutory exceptions of importance to education and librarianship. A few of them are examined in detail elsewhere in this book.

If your use is not "fair," don't forget the other statutory exceptions to the rights of owners. Fair use and the other exceptions apply independently of one another. You only need to comply with one of them to make your use lawful.

If your use is not within any of the exceptions, permission from the copyright owner is an important option. Indeed, unless you change your planned use of the copyrighted work, you might have little choice but to seek permission.

Fair use is relevant only if the work is protected by copyright. Do not overlook the possibility that the work you want to use may be in the public domain; if it is not protected by copyright, you do not have to worry about fair use. Similarly, if your use is not within the legal rights of the copyright owner, you are not an infringer, and you also do not have to consider fair use.

> A work may be in the public domain for many reasons. Two common reasons are that the copyright has expired, or the work was produced by the U.S. government. Much more about the public domain appears in chapters 2, 3, and 16.

Notes

1. *Copyright Law Revision*, 94th Cong., 2d sess., 1976, H. Doc. 1476.
2. The U.S. Supreme Court has stated clearly that fair use is a case-by-case determination. *Harper & Row Publishers, Inc. v. Nation Enterprises*, 471 U.S. 539, 549 (1985).
3. *U.S. Copyright Act*, 17 U.S.C. § 107 (2005).
4. *Folsom v. Marsh*, 9 F. Cas. 171 (C.C. Mass. 1841).
5. *U.S. Copyright Act of 1976*, Public Law 94-553, *U.S. Statutes at Large* 90 (1976): 2541, codified at 17 U.S.C. § 107 (2005).
6. *Campbell v. Acuff-Rose Music, Inc.*, 510 U.S. 569 (1994); *Kelly v. Arriba Soft Corp.*, 336 F.3d 811 (9th Cir. 2003); *Mattel, Inc. v. Walking Mountain Productions*, 353 F.3d 792 (9th Cir. 2004).
7. "Because this is not a mechanical determination, a party need not 'shut-out' her opponent on the four factor tally to prevail." *Wright v. Warner Books, Inc.*, 953 F.2d 731, 740 (2d Cir. 1991).
8. *Encyclopaedia Britannica Educational Corp. v. Crooks*, 542 F. Supp. 1156 (W.D.N.Y. 1982).
9. *Campbell v. Acuff-Rose Music, Inc.*, 510 U.S. 569.

8 Fair Use: Understanding the Four Factors

KEY POINTS

- *Purpose:* A nonprofit educational purpose can support a claim of fair use.

- *Nature:* Uses of factual, nonfiction works are more likely to be within fair use.

- *Amount:* The less the amount of a work used, the more likely it is fair use.

- *Effect:* Uses that do not compete with the market for the copyrighted work are more likely to be within fair use.

The determination of fair use depends on an application of the four factors in the statute—but before application must come careful definition of the meaning of each factor. Especially in the years since Congress adopted the first fair-use statute in 1976,[1] courts have handed down hundreds of decisions that give some meaning to the factors. The statute anticipates that other factors may enter into the decision about fair use.[2] In reality, however, courts rarely stray beyond the four factors set forth in the statute: *purpose, nature, amount,* and *effect.*

This chapter offers a general overview of the meaning and significance of the factors. Along the way, the focus will be on issues of special importance to educators and librarians. This overview will demonstrate that educational uses may be more favored by the fair-use doctrine, but "transformative" uses may be better—and they are increasingly common in education and research. The overview will also show that "less is more," but not always. The less you use of a work, the more likely it will be fair use, but using a limited amount still may be an infringement.

Confused? Don't be. You are beginning to discover the flexibility of the law, which is exactly the value of fair use as we seek to extend it to new needs and innovative situations.

Factor One: The Purpose and Character of the Use

The first factor examines whether the use of a copyrighted work "is of a commercial nature or is for nonprofit educational purposes."[3] With that crucial language, Congress explicitly signaled a favoring of nonprofit, educational uses over commercial uses. Photocopying for classroom handouts is more likely to be fair use than are copies for a professional meeting. Posting artwork on a website in connection with a research study is more likely to be fair use than is making the same copies for a commercial art catalog.

> One court found that a "thumbnail" image of a copyrighted photograph on the Internet constituted a "transformative" use because the image could not be enlarged and further reproduced by Internet users.
>
> —*Kelly v. Arriba Soft Corp.*, 336 F.3d 811 (9th Cir. 2003)

Fair use for education is common and of growing importance. With the expansion of "electronic reserves" and "course management systems" such as Blackboard and WebCT, instructors are creating files of readings and are easily posting the full text of articles, chapters, and other materials for students enrolled in various courses. For many of these situations, the key copyright question centers on fair use. At least on the basis of this first factor, educators should be able to make a strong argument for fair use. If the materials are directly related to the course, if they are posted only at the direction of the instructor, and if the passwords and other restrictions limit access only to students enrolled in that one course, then the claim of an "educational purpose" should be powerful and convincing.

> The simple act of password restriction will likely be important for the first factor and for the fourth factor. Limiting access can strengthen the argument that the materials are specifically for education; limiting access can also control the number of readers and risks of further duplication and dissemination of the copyrighted materials, which may help minimize the market harm and therefore strengthen the case for fair use.

Avoid jumping to conclusions. Your wonderful education or research use may still not be fair use. You may have an irrefutable argument on the first factor, but it might be outweighed by your application of the remaining three factors. Similarly, commercial needs are certainly not barred from the benefits of fair use.[4] Many for-profit entities have argued successfully for fair use. They may find that the first factor weighs against them, but the remaining three factors could yet tip the balance.

A single factor may also not be entirely for or against a finding of fair use. Some situations can create a mixed result on the first factor or any other. For example, when the U.S. Supreme Court considered whether a rap-parody version of a pop song could be fair use, the Court noted that the recording was a commercial product with considerable economic potential, but the use was also "criticism" or "commentary" for the purposes of fair use.[5] Those latter purposes are explicitly listed in the statute.

> Consider the critical case of *Salinger v. Random House, Inc.*, 811 F.2d 90 (2d Cir. 1987). Although the court ruled that the particular use in question was not fair use, the court did conclude that the first factor, on balance, weighed in favor of fair use. The use was, in one respect, for the commercial purpose of selling books for profit. But the court also found that the quotations from J. D. Salinger's correspondence were for the "research" purpose of writing biographical works. Overall, the first factor tipped in favor of fair use.

Transformative Uses

Courts also favor uses that are "transformative" or that are not mere reproductions.[6] Fair use is more likely when the copyrighted work is "transformed" into something new or of new utility. Examples might be quotations incorporated into a paper, or perhaps pieces of a work mixed into a multimedia product for your own teaching needs or included in commentary or criticism of the original. The notion of a "transformative" use is increasingly important to education and library work. As we develop multimedia tools and innovative online courses, we will be cutting and pasting, adding commentary, and exploring possibilities with images, text, and sound. Many of these uses may well be "transformative."

Multiple Copies

A teaching purpose gets one more important benefit in the law of fair use. Teaching is, of course, one of the favored purposes stated in the statute.[7] Along with that mention comes this specific language: "including multiple copies for classroom use."[8] For teaching purposes, multiple copies of some works are therefore specifically allowed, even if they are not "transformative." But be careful! This law does not mean that all copies for classroom handouts are fair use. You still need to evaluate and balance the three additional factors. You may, for example, conclude that photocopied handouts of a newspaper article are within the law, while also concluding that copies of book chapters in a coursepack are not fair use.

> In a 1994 decision, the U.S. Supreme Court emphasized the importance of "transformative" uses, but the Court pointedly noted that "the obvious statutory exception to this focus on transformative uses is the straight reproduction of multiple copies for classroom distribution."
>
> —*Campbell v. Acuff-Rose Music, Inc.*, 510 U.S. 569 (1994)

Factor Two: The Nature of the Copyrighted Work

This factor examines the characteristics and qualities of the copyrighted work being used. The underlying concept is that some works are more appropriate for fair use, while fair use applies more narrowly to other types of works.[9] The "nature of the work" requires an examination of the qualities and attributes of the copyrighted work you are using, and inferring whether the work is of a type that merits greater protection and less fair use—or is the kind of work that fair use is meant for us to build upon to expand the growth and dissemination of knowledge.

Courts have had occasion to draw some lines demonstrating this point. For example, several court decisions have concluded that the unpublished "nature" of historical correspondence can weigh against fair use.[10] The courts have reasoned that copyright owners should have the right to determine the circumstances of "first publication" and whether, when, and how to make the works publicly available. When courts find that a work has been published, they tend to be more lenient with fair use.

Other examples of judicial line drawing with regard to the second factor can be helpful and have proved important for the work of educators and librarians.

> In 1985 the U.S. Supreme Court ruled in *Harper & Row Publishers, Inc. v. Nation Enterprises* that fair use applied narrowly to an unpublished book manuscript, in order to preserve the "right of first publication" for the copyright owner. Where did this "right" come from, and what does it mean? Chapter 16 offers some insights. That chapter also traces the series of rulings about historical manuscripts that the *Harper & Row* decision spawned. Confusion about this issue eventually led Congress to modify the fair-use statute.

Fiction and Nonfiction

Fair use generally applies more generously to published works of nonfiction. Articles, books, and other works of nonfiction—whether about mathematics, biology, politics, or any other subject—are exactly the types of works for which fair use can have the most meaning. Why? Because the central purpose of copyright law, including fair use, is to allow for the growth of knowledge.[11] To accomplish that goal, we regularly need to use and build upon earlier works. Most often, these efforts depend on using the nonfiction works of earlier scholarship. Courts have recognized this reality.

By contrast, the law gives greater protection—and allows less fair use—for works of fiction.[12] Fair use will be relatively constrained for clips of novels, poetry, and stage plays. You will likely find a similar outcome for uses of other more creative materials, such as art, photography, music, and motion pictures. This rule does not mean that fair use vaporizes. It simply means that the second factor will be more easily construed against a finding of fair use for such works. To compensate in the overall balance, you may need to strengthen the arguments for fair use on the other factors.

Consumable and "Out of Print"

Other principles can help bring practical meaning to the "nature" factor. For example, this factor may weigh against fair use when applied to copies of workbook pages and excerpts from other "consumable" materials. Publishers often produce and sell workbooks with the expectation that they will be fully consumed and repurchased with each use. Copies can undermine the copyright owner's expectations.[13]

> The example of consumable works is another good demonstration of one "fact" being important to the evaluation of more than one "factor." In evaluating the fair use of a workbook, for example, you might conclude that the "nature" factor leans against fair use. Because the copies would also interfere with the continuous marketing of the workbook to students, you might find that the fourth factor, the "effect on the market," also weighs against fair use.

A more complicated, but common, circumstance has split the authorities. Many copyrighted works go "out of print," even though the copyright may live on for decades. A U.S. Senate report from 1975, and one early case, asserted that if a work is out of print, copying may not harm the market.[14] After all, the copyright owner is not actively claiming a market and seeking sales.

A well-known ruling against the Kinko's photocopying chain in 1991 picked up on a nuance of this principle, finding that the copyright owners of out-of-print materials in that case were in fact offering a license to make copies. That court reasoned that even though a work is out of print, copies of it can still interfere with the marketing of a license to make copies.[15] The court further found that licensing is the primary remaining market for such a work, so the copies may cause a more profound economic harm.[16]

What can you conclude from these cases? Perhaps the main point is that you may often need to investigate the realistic and current marketing of the work you want to use. If it is actively licensed, you might be affecting that market. If the copyright owner has not made reasonable arrangements for licensing, "out of print" may lead to broader fair use.

> Notice again that one fact—in this case the fact that a work is out of print—can become important in the evaluation of two factors: the "nature" factor and the "effect" factor.

Factor Three: The Amount and Substantiality of the Portion Used

The "amount" factor perhaps sounds like it should be reasonably straightforward. No such luck. The "amount" used of a work is measured both quantitatively and qualitatively.[17] No exact measures of allowable quantity exist in the law. Furthermore, rules about word counts and percentages have no place in the law of fair use. At best, they are interpretations intended to streamline fair use;

at worst, they erode the flexibility that makes fair use meaningful in new situations. Quantity must be evaluated relative to the length of the entire original work and the amount needed to serve a proper "purpose." Amount must also be viewed in light of the "nature" of the work being used.

> One court cautioned that even fleeting images of artistic works in a television production might not tip the "amount" factor sufficiently toward fair use to outweigh other factors.
>
> —*Ringgold v. Black Entertainment Television, Inc.,* 126 F.3d 70 (2d Cir. 1997)

Some works are appropriate only for more extensive uses. One court has ruled that a journal article alone is an entire work, and copying an entire work, at least in a commercial setting, usually weighs heavily against fair use.[18] The next chapter offers a closer look at that ruling and other cases struggling with the copying of book chapters and other significant portions of textual works. Pictures generate serious controversies in regard to this factor, because a user nearly always wants the full image or the entire "amount." Yet courts have reckoned with copies that are of the full image, but are "thumbnail" size or are of low resolution.[19] The copying may be "quantitatively" large, but may be "qualitatively" limited.

> Chapter 9 summarizes court cases holding that full articles and sizable excerpts from books are beyond the limits of the allowed "amount." Those cases were brought against for-profit companies that could not convince the courts that they had a favored "purpose." The outcome of the analysis can shift greatly if the purpose is for nonprofit education or research.

Quantity and Quality

The tension between "quantitative" and "qualitative" measures is most vividly demonstrated by the concept of using the "heart of the work." In the *Harper & Row* case in 1985, the Supreme Court analyzed whether *The Nation* magazine had exceeded fair use when it quoted some 300 words from Pres. Gerald Ford's then-unpublished memoir into a news article. The Court ruled that while the quotations might be quantitatively small, they were the pieces of the book that a reader would likely find most interesting and were therefore the "heart" of the manuscript. The Court reasoned that the "amount" factor thus weighed against fair use.[20]

> Sometimes copying the full work can be within fair use. A company copied an entire software program made for a Sony Playstation in order to reverse engineer it and create an emulator. The court ruled that the "amount" factor weighed only slightly against fair use, because the Sony program never became part of the new emulator.
>
> —*Sony Computer Entertainment, Inc. v. Connectix Corp.,* 203 F.3d 596 (9th Cir. 2000)

Motion pictures are also problematic because even short clips may borrow the most extraordinary or creative elements in them. One may reproduce only a small portion of any work but still take "the heart of the work." The "substantiality" concept represents such a qualitative measure that may weigh against fair use.

Practical Sense

How do you make reliable and practical sense of the "amount" factor? Indeed, shorter excerpts from works are more likely than longer pieces to be within fair use. Frankly, in most situations, that one simple rule is likely to be the most important one. Yet sometimes even the briefest slice may constitute the "heart of the work." You can strengthen your claim of fair use by tying the "amount" to the educational or research "purpose" identified with respect to the first factor. If you can meet your needs with only excerpts of the article or movie, you are best advised to clip and share only those elements. But if you absolutely have to have the entire work, be sure you have a strong "purpose" argument and are ready to relate the use of the full work to meeting clear needs.

Bear in mind that even if you are copying the "whole article" or digitizing the crucial chariot race from *Ben Hur* (perhaps the "heart" of the film), this factor is only one of four factors that must be balanced together to reach a conclusion. Even if this factor weighs against fair use, your use may still be fair.

Factor Four: The Effect of the Use on the Market

Effect on the market is perhaps even more complicated than the other three factors. Some courts have called it the most important factor, although that statement is difficult to justify.[21] This factor fundamentally means that if you make a use for which a purchase of an original theoretically should have occurred—regardless of your personal willingness or ability to pay for such purchase—this factor may weigh against fair use. Occasional quotations or photocopies may pose little significant market harm, but full reproductions of software and videotapes can make direct inroads on the potential market for those works.

> The U.S. Supreme Court, in the *Harper & Row* case, called the "effect" factor "most important." Realistically, though, one can see that in applying fair use narrowly to an unpublished book manuscript, the Court put at least comparable weight on the unpublished "nature" of the work (i.e., the second factor). Many other cases have cited that language from the Supreme Court, but a close reading suggests that those courts are also just giving added weight to the factors that have greatest prominence under the given facts.

The easy cases occur when the use directly replaces a potential sale of the copyrighted work. One court has ruled that downloading music from the original, free version of Napster substituted for sales of CDs, and so found demonstrable market harm.[22] In the lawsuit against Kinko's, another court ruled that when Kinko's made and sold copies of book chapters, the company eliminated any realistic likelihood that students would ever buy those books.[23] Harder cases involve uses that do not interfere with simple sales, but might undercut licensing. The photocopying of isolated articles might not replace subscriptions to the entire journal, but the copying might interfere with the system of permissions and collection of fees put in place by the publisher or other rights holders.[24]

> Chapter 9 includes a summary of *American Geophysical Union v. Texaco Inc.* The court ruled that the existence of systems for the relatively easy licensing of rights to make copies of journal articles established a market that the user was harming. This case, and the licensing system, are examined more fully in chapter 9.

Consider the many ways that market "effect" can vary greatly. You find a document properly made available on the Internet. The copyright owner clearly has imposed no restrictions or conditions on access and is asserting no claim to payment for use. You copy, download, or print the materials in full. You have probably done nothing to harm any realistic market. In another situation, you are creating a document that you want to post on a website. You want to include in your document sizable quotations and copies of various charts and images from other sources. The "effect" factor may again support the application of fair use, because moving those pieces into a new project and embedding them in the context of an analytical study are not likely to interfere with a realistic market. The more you alter the context of use and surround the works with original criticism or comment, the less you are likely impeding a market that the copyright owner can control.

Chapter 11 examines the TEACH Act for distance learning. While that law is not at all the same as "fair use," it does include some analogous concepts. For example, the TEACH Act explicitly does not allow uses of materials that are marketed for digital distance education. Fair use has no such bar. On the other hand, the fact that the owners are targeting a specialized market means that such a use is more likely to harm the defined market—and hence less likely to be within fair use.

These issues are challenging for courts, too, and they have devised some shortcuts for applying the "effect" factor. For example, this factor is closely linked to "purpose." If your purpose is research or scholarship, market harm may be difficult to prove, and courts will generally apply the factor somewhat generously. If your purpose is commercial, however, some harm to the market is presumed.[25] Still, one can imagine that the rules become blurred when you have an "educational" purpose, but the work you are using is one that is created and marketed especially for the academic community. The hard reality is that even some educational uses have direct and adverse market consequences.

Market issues can get complicated, but in the context of fair use they ultimately drive this line of thinking: How is the work actually marketed? What are the realistic potential markets? Is the work realistically marketed for my needs and my uses? Am I harming or inhibiting that market potential? Am I replacing a sale? Are my market effects significant? Would they be significant if uses like mine were widespread?

Do not overlook that your use might actually *help* the market for the work. References, clips, quotations, images, and other such uses invariably draw attention to the original work. In some cases these uses might take away a market. In other cases, the use might lead someone to want more and to make a purchase. Quotations in a book review are a familiar example of a use that probably helps the market for a work.

Like almost all matters of applying fair use, this fourth factor depends on an array of facts. Those facts may be the circumstances of your use, and they are most certainly about the active or likely marketing of the work you plan to use. You clearly need to have a firm grasp of your situation, and you must investigate facts about the work in question. You might also find that markets change. A work may have no market today, but find a new market tomorrow. A work may be a best seller this year, but be out of print in the near future. Testing the market might also mean retesting it again in future applications of fair use.

Notes

1. *U.S. Copyright Act of 1976*, Public Law 94-553, *U.S. Statutes at Large* 90 (1976): 2541, codified at 17 *U.S.C.* § 107 (2005).
2. The use of the word "include" when listing factors of fair use in the statute denotes that the factors listed are not an exclusive list. *U.S. Copyright Act*, 17 *U.S.C.* § 107 (2005).
3. *U.S. Copyright Act*, 17 *U.S.C.* § 107.
4. "A commercial use weighs against a finding of fair use but is not conclusive on the issue." *A&M Records, Inc. v. Napster, Inc.*, 239 F.3d 1004 (9th Cir. 2001).
5. *Campbell v. Acuff-Rose Music, Inc.*, 510 U.S. 569, 593 (1994).
6. Under this factor, courts often ask whether the new work merely replaces the object of the original creation "or instead adds something new, with a further purpose or different character, altering the first with new expression, meaning, or message; it asks, in other words, whether and to what extent the new work is 'transformative.'" *Campbell v. Acuff-Rose Music, Inc.*, 510 U.S. 569, 579.
7. *U.S. Copyright Act*, 17 *U.S.C.* § 107.
8. *U.S. Copyright Act*, 17 *U.S.C.* § 107.

9. This factor calls for recognition that some works are closer to the "core of intended copyright protection" than others, with the consequence that fair use is more difficult to establish when the former works are copied. *Campbell v. Acuff-Rose Music, Inc.*, 510 U.S. 569, 586.

10. *Harper & Row Publishers, Inc. v. Nation Enterprises*, 471 U.S. 539 (1985); *NXIVM Corp. v. Ross Institute*, 364 F.3d 471, 480 (2d Cir. 2004).

11. U.S. Constitution, art. I, sec. 8, cl. 8.

12. *Campbell v. Acuff-Rose Music, Inc.*, 510 U.S. 569, 586.

13. *Copyright Law Revision*, 94th Cong., 2d sess., 1976. H. Doc. 1476.

14. *Copyright Law Revision*, 94th Cong., 1st sess., 1975. S. Doc. 473; *Maxtone-Graham v. Burtchaell*, 803 F.2d 1253 (2d Cir. 1986).

15. *Basic Books, Inc. v. Kinko's Graphics Corp.*, 758 F. Supp. 1522 (S.D.N.Y. 1991).

16. *Basic Books, Inc., v. Kinko's Graphics Corp.*, 758 F. Supp. 1522.

17. *Campbell v. Acuff-Rose Music, Inc.*, 510 U.S. 569, 587; *Elvis Presley Enterprises, Inc. v. Passport Video*, 349 F.3d 622, 630 (9th Cir. 2003).

18. *American Geophysical Union v. Texaco Inc.*, 60 F.3d 913 (2d Cir. 1994).

19. *Kelly v. Arriba Soft Corp.*, 336 F.3d 811 (9th Cir. 2003).

20. *Harper & Row Publishers, Inc. v. Nation Enterprises*, 471 U.S. 539, 564–566 (1985).

21. *Harper & Row Publishers, Inc. v. Nation Enterprises*, 471 U.S. 539, 566.

22. *A&M Records, Inc. v. Napster, Inc.*, 239 F.3d 1004 (9th Cir. 2001).

23. *Basic Books, Inc. v. Kinko's Graphics Corp.*, 758 F. Supp. 1522 (S.D.N.Y. 1991).

24. *American Geophysical Union v. Texaco Inc.*, 60 F.3d 913 (2d Cir. 1994).

25. *Harper & Row Publishers, Inc. v. Nation Enterprises*, 471 U.S. 539.

9 Getting Comfortable with Fair Use: Applying the Four Factors

---

KEY POINTS

- ■ Few court rulings about fair use are directly applicable to education and libraries.

- ■ A variety of other court rulings concerning fair use offer important guidance for teaching and research.

- ■ Fair use ultimately depends on a balancing of the four factors in the statute as applied to specific facts.

- ■ We can begin to discern the meaning of fair use for many common needs.

American courts have analyzed and applied fair use in hundreds or thousands of cases, but rarely have they interpreted fair use for educational or library activities. A growing number of colleges, universities, libraries, and other organizations may face accusations of copyright infringement, or may be analyzing and applying fair use to innovative projects, but seldom do the situations progress—or degenerate—into lawsuits. The parties settle; the questionable activities stop; the project rarely stirs legal anxieties.

Whatever the reason, the matter is resolved long before a judge has a chance to tell us what the law really is. Consequently, those of us working in the field of education and librarianship are left to infer what we can from the few cases that have some relevance. Courts have expounded on fair use in several cases that offer analogous situations.

A prime example involves Kinko's, which was sued years ago for making photocopied course-packs without permission.[1] The court rejected the defense of fair use, in large part because Kinko's was a for-profit entity, photocopying for a commercial purpose. Imagine a similar case, not against Kinko's, but against a university. Copying for nonprofit, educational purposes may sway the first factor in the opposite direction. A court may well find that some copying in the hands of the educational institution could be fair use. But we do not have that case. We can only use our best judgment and infer the law's possible meaning.

The author of this book has written on several other occasions about the significance of the *Kinko's* case. For his opinion about the meaning of the case in the educational setting, written shortly after the court handed down its ruling, see Kenneth D. Crews, "Federal Court's Ruling against Photocopying Chain Will Not Destroy 'Fair Use,'" *Chronicle of Higher Education*, April 17, 1991, A48.

Courts are also slowly beginning to address the fair use of diverse media. In *Higgins v. Detroit Educational Broadcasting Foundation*, the court allowed as fair use the incorporation of short pieces of a musical work into the background of a video production that was broadcast on a local PBS affiliate and sold in limited copies to educational institutions.[2] The court sympathized with the educational and public-service "purpose" of the production. The defendant used a brief "amount"—only about thirty-five seconds of a popular song—and only in the background of the opening scenes. A song is generally a creative work, so the "nature" factor tipped in favor of stronger protection and against fair use. The song was not actively licensed for such uses, so the use had no adverse "market effect." Three of the four factors weighed in favor of fair use, and the court ruled accordingly.

Other decisions reveal the limits of fair use. Consider these conclusions from various courts:

- The full text of newspaper articles posted to an unrestricted website—even to further a social cause—is not fair use.[3]

- Playing music in the background while phone callers are placed "on hold" is not fair use.[4]

- Glimpses of photographs in the background of a movie or television production have left courts seemingly divided. One court ruled that if the images are fairly prominent in the set for a cable TV show, they are not fair use.[5] Another court ruled that fuzzy images in a motion picture scene are fair use.[6]

- Uploading and downloading music files through the original Napster is not within fair use.[7]

Still, none of these cases exactly addresses the common needs of education, research, and librarianship. Courts have not ruled on questions of classroom handouts, library reserves, online courses, and digital libraries. Nevertheless, we need to decide if these activities are within fair use—even without explicit guidance from the law.

This chapter offers guidance for thinking about fair use in a variety of situations, ranging from familiar needs to legally unresolved territory. This chapter demonstrates the practical application of fair use in order to meet important objectives. It offers simple scenarios that are at the core of common practice among educators and librarians. The scenarios begin with the simplest and build to larger-scale projects and newer technologies. The principal point of each scenario is to model the process of thinking through the four factors and moving toward a conclusion about fair use.

Quoting in Publications

SCENARIO

Professor Tran is writing a lengthy historical study and wants to include in it various quotations and clips of other copyrighted materials. Is she protected by fair use?

Of course, whether or not Professor Tran is staying within the boundaries of the law will depend on a multitude of variables, but start with the most familiar situation and move to the more complex. Begin with simply quoting from one work into her new historical study. To help us through the four factors, we can find some relevant cases, such as *Penelope v. Brown*.[8]

In that case, a professor, Penelope, wrote a book about English grammar and language usage. Brown, a writer of popular fiction, later wrote a manual for budding authors. Amidst five pages of Brown's 218-page book, she apparently copied sentence examples from Penelope's work. When Penelope sued, the court ruled that Brown's use was fair. Here is how the court addressed the four factors:

> The notion of a "productive" use is a breed of the "transformative" use examined in chapter 8. Courts are more generous with fair use when the new work "transforms" the original and gives it a new purpose or function—or if the use builds on the original in some "productive" manner. In either instance, the court is allowing greater fair use in order to "promote the progress" of knowledge and creativity.

Purpose: The court found that the second book greatly expanded on pieces borrowed from the first, making the use "productive." The court also found little commercial character in the use of the small excerpts, and it found no improper conduct by Brown. This factor favors fair use.

Nature: The court looked to the nonfiction "nature" of the work used and its limited availability to the public. This factor favors fair use.

Amount: The excerpts were a small "amount" of the first work. This factor favors fair use.

Effect: The court found little adverse "effect" on the market for the original, noting that the two books might appear side by side in a store, but a buyer would not be likely to see one as a replacement for the other. This factor also favors fair use.

The *Penelope* case might give Professor Tran considerable peace of mind if she is using short quotations from a published, nonfiction work. The one case, however, does not tell how far Tran can go. What about long quotations? What if she were not copying published text, but instead pictures, poetry, unpublished manuscripts, or other types of works?

The case of *Maxtone-Graham v. Burtchaell* suggests how Professor Tran might test the limits of the law with lengthy quotations.[9] In 1973 an author wrote a book based on interviews with women about their own pregnancies and abortions. Sometime later, another author prepared his own book on the same subject and sought permission to use lengthy excerpts from the first work. The first author, the plaintiff in this case, refused permission, and the defendant proceeded to publish his work with the unpermitted excerpts. The borrowed material encompassed more than 4.3 percent of the plaintiff's work, including many insightful passages from the interviews. The court relied on the four factors to determine whether the lengthy quoting was fair use.

> Notice that the user of the original work first sought permission—often a good approach. But the request was also denied—often a common result. Even so, fair use was possible. Sometimes the denial of permission can mean that fair use is the only means for using the work, and courts seem to be especially sympathetic if the use has some social good, such as examining important issues.

Purpose: The defendant's book was published by a commercial press with the possibility of monetary success, but the main purpose of the book was to educate the public about abortion and about the author's views. This factor favors fair use.

Nature: The interviews were largely factual, which also favors fair use.

Amount: Quoting 4.3 percent of the plaintiff's work was not excessive, and the verbatim passages were not necessarily central to the plaintiff's book. Again, this factor supports fair use.

Effect: The court found no significant threat to the plaintiff's market. Indeed, the court noted that the plaintiff's work was out of print and not likely to appeal to the same readers.

If lengthy quotations can be within fair use, then would using large portions of copyrighted works in the context of teaching materials also be okay? Consider the case of *Marcus v. Rowley*.[10] A schoolteacher prepared a 24-page pamphlet on cake decorating for her adult education classes. Eleven of those pages were taken directly from a copyrighted pamphlet prepared by another teacher. Even though both pamphlets were of limited circulation and were for teaching purposes only, the court held that the copying was not fair use. Important factors in this case were that the copying was a substantial part of the original pamphlet; that the copying embraced the original pamphlet's most significant portions; and that the second pamphlet competed directly with the original pamphlet's educational purpose. Our fictitious Professor Tran could be in trouble if she copies extensive materials that are created specifically to serve a competing educational market.

The *Marcus* case tells much about limits on simple copying, but the *Maxtone-Graham* case affirms that quotations in a subsequent work are permissible, sometimes even when they are extensive. This case also suggests much about using materials in an educational setting, where an instructor may be using pieces and clips of various works to prepare teaching materials or an online course. Even large pieces could be within fair use, especially for the favored purpose of education. Fair use is also stronger if the instructor is using the materials in the context of overall original teaching materials and with accompanying comments and criticism.

What if the user is doing more than merely copying pieces and embedding them in a larger and original publication? What if Professor Tran is looking to copy materials in full without original commentary? The next cases shed some light on straight copying.

Copying for Coursepacks

SCENARIO
Professor Tran teaches at a community college and wants to make photocopies of articles and book excerpts as handouts for her students. Is she within fair use?

American courts have yet to rule on the question of fair use for paper or electronic copies made for educational purposes. But two cases from the 1990s examined fair use for commercial photocopying, and they offer some analogous insights. The first case is the landmark ruling in *Basic Books, Inc. v. Kinko's Graphics Corp.*[11]

Kinko's was held to be infringing copyrights when it photocopied book chapters for sale to students as "coursepacks" for their university classes.

> The publishers in the *Kinko's* case urged the court to rule that any "anthology" or coursepack could not be allowed under fair use. The court rejected that contention, concluding instead that one must analyze each article, chapter, or other work separately and determine whether each item in the coursepack is within the law.

Purpose: When conducted by Kinko's, the copying was for commercial purposes, and not for educational purposes. Therefore, this factor weighs against fair use.

Nature: Most of the works were factual—they were works of history, sociology, and other fields of study. This factor tips in favor of fair use.

Amount: The court analyzed the percentage used of each work, finding that copying 5 to 25 percent of the original full book was excessive. This factor tips against fair use.

Effect: The court found a direct adverse effect on the market for the books, because the coursepacks competed with the potential sales of the original books as assigned reading for the students. The photocopying of selected chapters realistically undercut sales of the books to those students, tipping this factor against fair use.

Three of the four factors leaned against fair use. The court held that Kinko's therefore had committed infringement.

The second case is *Princeton University Press v. Michigan Document Services, Inc.*[12] A private copy shop created and sold "coursepacks" under circumstances similar to those in *Kinko's*, and the copy shop was also found to have acted outside the limits of fair use. This case sharply divided the panel of appellate judges who ruled on it. Nevertheless, the court's reasoning was similar to the *Kinko's* decision, with at least one important difference: the court gave most of its attention to the question of market harm. The court was particularly persuaded by the availability of options for licensing the materials—or securing permission from the copyright owners—before making the copies. The court also noted that securing permissions had become standard procedure among commercial shops making photocopied coursepacks.

The *Princeton* case attracted strong attention from the academic community when the court of appeals first ruled that the copying indeed was within fair use. The publishers promptly appealed to the full panel of thirteen judges of the Sixth Circuit Court of Appeals. Even on that final review, only eight judges concluded that the copying was not fair use. Five judges dissented, finding that the copying should be allowed. If experienced judges disagree about the law, we should not be surprised when educators and librarians also debate the scope and application of fair use.

What do these cases tell us about Professor Tran's needs? She has a definite advantage when she makes the copies herself on the college's own machines, thereby avoiding the disfavored commercial purpose. She can also help her cause by keeping the materials that she copies as brief as possible and perhaps by checking the market for the reasonable availability of permission from the copyright owner.

What if Professor Tran wants to post the materials to a secured website or distribute them to students on a CD-ROM? Fundamentally, fair use applies to electronic uses just as it does to paper copies. However, digital copies are easily copied, uploaded, and shared without realistic limits. To help her case for fair use, Professor Tran should restrict access to the materials by means of password protections or other controls, and she should take the occasion to help her students understand the copyright implications of any misuse.

Single Copies for Research

SCENARIO
Professor Tran needs to make single copies of articles, chapters, and other materials to support her research or to help her prepare for teaching. Are individual copies within fair use?

In general, single, isolated copies of brief items should easily fall within fair use. In the context of nonprofit education and research, they are probably within the law. The case of *American Geophysical Union v. Texaco Inc.,* however, is a reminder that the limits of fair use can arise in the seemingly most innocuous circumstances.[13] The case involved the photocopying of individual journal articles by a Texaco scientist for his own research needs. The court held that the copying was not within fair use.

> In an unusual development, the court amended its opinion in the *Texaco* case several months after its original issuance, adding language that limited the ruling to "systematic" copying that may advance the profit goals of the larger organization. Apparently, the judges were still debating the wisdom of the ruling long after issuing it.

Purpose: While research is generally a favored purpose, the ultimate purpose was to strengthen Texaco's corporate profits. Moreover, exact photocopies are not "transformative"; they do not build on the existing work in a productive manner.

Nature: The articles were factual, which weighs in favor of fair use.

Amount: An article is an independent work, so copying the article is copying the entire copyrighted work. This factor weighs against fair use.

Effect: The court found no evidence that Texaco reasonably would have purchased more subscriptions to the relevant journals if it had not copied them, but the court did conclude that unpermitted photocopying directly competes with the ability of publishers to collect license fees. According to the court, the Copyright Clearance Center (CCC) provides a practical method for paying fees and securing permissions, so the copying directly undercut the ability to pursue the market for licensing through the CCC.

> Chapter 17 provides guidance and insight about seeking permissions, and it includes additional information about the role and function of the Copyright Clearance Center.

Despite an impassioned dissent from one judge who argued for the realistic needs of researchers, the court found three of the four factors weighing against fair use in the corporate context. This case was a clear signal to many for-profit entities that they ought to consider securing licenses that cover their copying and other uses of many copyrighted works. This is especially true because the CCC offers a "blanket license" at one annual fee for many corporate clients.

For nonprofit users, the case is a dose of caution about simple photocopying, although a court is not likely to construe fair use so narrowly in that context. The *Texaco* decision emphasizes that the ruling applies only to "systematic" commercial copying, and the court explicitly noted that it would not likely extend the ruling to individual researchers acting solely at their own behest for their own research initiatives. Our fictitious Professor Tran is likely to conclude that much of her copying of single, brief items is fair use. She would likely reach the same conclusion about single downloads and printouts from the Internet or from electronic databases.

Cutting and Pasting for Multimedia Projects

SCENARIO
Professor Tran wants to create an innovative teaching tool by cutting and pasting a variety of works into a single cohesive set of materials for the students enrolled in her classes. She might place a CD-ROM of her project in the library collection for the local students, and she might post her project to a secured website for students enrolled in her course through distance education.

If the "multimedia" tool that Professor Tran is creating is little more than copies of reading and other materials, then her analysis of fair use may be much like the scenarios involving coursepacks. She is generally just making a digital version of the familiar print materials. Similarly, if she is clipping pieces and excerpts of materials, arranging them in an innovative manner, and enveloping them with original commentary and instructional content, then she may be making a high-tech version of a book or teaching materials.

In either event, the question of fair use will turn on the circumstances surrounding each individual item. If she is using clips of nonfiction text, fair use should be reasonably flexible. If she is using music, art, poetry, and other more creative works, she should be more constrained. If she is wrapping the use in commentary and criticism, she is on safer ground than she would be with straight copying.

Perhaps most significant for Professor Tran, she can strengthen her claim of fair use by tightly limiting access to the students enrolled in her course. Her options for controlling access are limited only by imagination and opportunity. Professor Tran has many high-tech and low-tech options for restricting access. Among the possibilities:

- The CD-ROM may be available in the library, but only students in the course are allowed to check it out.

- She might make a few copies of the CD-ROM and distribute them directly to students, but admonish them against additional copies or other misuse.

- She might install the content on a network server that has password controls, allowing only enrolled students to retrieve the materials.

> As the scenario unfolds, Professor Tran is developing a multimedia teaching tool that students may be able to access on the Internet or other delivery system. The scenario is starting to have the look of a modern distance-learning course. Fair use can allow instructors to copy, upload, and transmit materials in distance education. The TEACH Act is a new law that does not replace fair use, but instead offers an alternative set of rules for using copyrighted works in distance education. For more about the TEACH Act, see chapter 11.

A few recent court cases remind us that one can still face limits on fair use, even in a controlled, academic setting.

In *Los Angeles Times v. Free Republic*, the court ruled that posting the full text of newspaper articles to a website is not fair use.[14] Professor Tran, by contrast, is proposing to use materials for non-profit education and only with restricted access. She can strengthen the possibilities of fair use by using only excerpts of articles. She can avoid issues of fair use entirely by linking to databases that might be available from her library and that include the materials she wants her students to read.

In *Tiffany Design, Inc. v. Reno-Tahoe Specialty, Inc.*, the court ruled that digital cutting and pasting of photographic elements into an innovative montage of the Las Vegas skyline was not fair use.[15] The purpose was to create a commercial product for sale to the public. Professor Tran, by contrast, is producing teaching materials only to serve her instructional needs. Notice that should she decide to publish her creative materials as a commercial product, she likely needs to anticipate a contraction of fair use.

In *NXIVM Corp. v. Ross Institute*, the court ruled that fair use could allow someone to produce a critical analysis of copyrighted materials used in business seminars.[16] Fair use allowed the defendant to make a critical analysis of the materials and to post that critique on the Internet—even if it included approximately seventeen pages from the 500 pages in the original materials. The court was especially inclined to allow substantial copying and public accessibility when the use was in the context of original criticism and analysis. This case is important reassurance to Professor Tran, if she is not simply making straight copies, but is including selected excerpts amidst original teaching materials.

Flexibility of Fair Use

As Professor Tran pursues a range of activities, from simple quoting to creating innovative teaching materials, she is steadily encountering questions about fair use. The answer is always: "it depends." The most important good news is that fair use is flexible. Fair use can apply in all of these situations and more. It can apply to a full range of materials, from text and software to music and art. Fair use has enormous potential to support Professor Tran's work.

> When Congress enacted the fair-use statute in 1976, it recognized that educators and librarians would need to make difficult judgments about fair use. The Copyright Act therefore includes some important protection for these users who act in good faith as they strive to learn about and apply fair use. Chapter 13 provides the details.

The flexibility of fair use can also make it challenging as well as frustrating. The flexibility of fair use also means that it has no clear, firm, and established limits. It is variable in its scope, and its meaning is always open to debate. The next chapter examines the "guidelines" that have attempted to bring some clarity to the law. In the process, however, they have also done considerable harm to the greatest virtues of fair use: its flexibility and its adaptability to new situations and new demands.

Acting in Good Faith

Should Professor Tran actually work with the factors of fair use and make a well-reasoned decision, the law will give her an important reward. As she works through the issues, Professor Tran is likely to feel a burden of responsibility and an accompanying risk of legal liability. Indeed, chapter 13 of this book will tell of the severe consequences that may befall an infringer of someone's copyrighted work. Congress recognized that educators and libraries face this dilemma. The law therefore includes an important provision that eliminates much of the financial liability Professor Tran could face, but she will have that advantage only if she applies the law of fair use in a reasonable and good-faith manner.

Chapter 13 will offer more details, but for now the message is clear: if Professor Tran learns and applies the factors of fair use, she can have the benefit of greatly reduced liability. But do not overlook the better and more direct message: if Professor Tran learns and applies the factors of fair use, she is also very likely acting within the law and may face no liability at all.

Notes

1. *Basic Books, Inc. v. Kinko's Graphics Corp.*, 758 F. Supp. 1522 (S.D.N.Y. 1991).
2. *Higgins v. Detroit Educational Broadcasting Foundation*, 4 F. Supp. 2d 701 (E.D. Mich. 1998).
3. *Los Angeles Times v. Free Republic*, 54 U.S.P.Q.2d 1862 (C.D. Cal. 2000).
4. *Infinity Broadcasting Corp. v. Kirkwood*, 63 F. Supp. 2d 420 (S.D.N.Y. 1999).
5. *Ringgold v. Black Entertainment Television, Inc.*, 126 F.3d 70 (2d Cir. 1997).
6. *Sandoval v. New Line Cinema Corp.*, 147 F.3d 215 (2d Cir. 1998).
7. *A&M Records, Inc. v. Napster, Inc.*, 239 F.3d 1004 (9th Cir. 2001).
8. *Penelope v. Brown*, 792 F. Supp. 132 (D. Mass. 1992).
9. *Maxtone-Graham v. Burtchaell*, 803 F.2d 1253 (2d Cir. 1986), *cert. denied*, 481 U.S. 1059 (1987).
10. *Marcus v. Rowley*, 695 F.2d 1171 (9th Cir. 1983).
11. *Basic Books, Inc. v. Kinko's Graphics Corp.*, 758 F. Supp. 1522 (S.D.N.Y. 1991).
12. *Princeton University Press v. Michigan Document Services*, 99 F.3d 1381 (6th Cir. 1996), *cert. denied*, 520 U.S. 1156 (1997).
13. *American Geophysical Union v. Texaco Inc.*, 60 F.3d 913 (2d Cir. 1994), *cert. dismissed*, 516 U.S. 1005 (1995).
14. *Los Angeles Times v. Free Republic*, 54 U.S.P.Q.2d 1862 (C.D. Cal. 2000).
15. *Tiffany Design, Inc. v. Reno-Tahoe Specialty, Inc.*, 55 F. Supp. 2d 1113 (D. Nev. 1999).
16. *NXIVM Corp. v. Ross Institute*, 364 F.3d 471 (2d Cir. 2004).

10

The Meaning of Fair-Use Guidelines

KEY POINTS

- Various groups have developed guidelines that apply fair use to diverse situations.

- Even though your use may not fit within the guidelines, your use may still be fair use.

- The guidelines may be helpful for some needs, but users must remember that guidelines are not the law.

- Only by returning to the four factors can one have the full benefit of fair use.

When courts developed the law of fair use, and when Congress enacted the first fair-use statute in 1976, they made clear that the law of fair use was never intended to anticipate specific answers for individual situations. Indeed, Congress acted deliberately to assure that it would not "freeze" the doctrine of fair use by giving it a narrowly defined meaning. As a result, the law calls on each of us to apply a set of factors to each situation. Because of the variability of the law, reasonable people can and will disagree about the meaning of fair use in even the most common applications.

Evolution of Guidelines

Educators, librarians, and others had expressed great concern about the possible ambiguity of fair use even before Congress enacted the first fair-use statute in 1976. Congress made clear that it would not make the law more specific, and it urged interested parties to meet privately and to negotiate shared understandings of fair use. The result was a series of guidelines that attempt to define fair use as applied to common situations. The first of these guidelines emerged in 1976 on the issues of photocopying for classroom handouts and the copying of music.

Through the years, various groups have devised guidelines on other issues, from off-air video-taping to library copies. In the 1990s, such guidelines gained renewed prominence with the formation of the Conference on Fair Use (CONFU). CONFU was an outgrowth of the National Information Infrastructure initiative under the Clinton administration, and it involved participation from a broad range of interests: teachers, librarians, industry and government officials, and many others. The final report from CONFU proposed three more guidelines for newer technological issues.

> The preceding chapters of this book offer a detailed look at the law of fair use. One prominent characteristic of fair use is its flexibility. Flexibility allows fair use to apply to many new needs and situations, but it also requires users to make judgments about the law that are sometimes difficult and discomforting.

Major Guidelines, 1976–1998

Various groups have issued guidelines since 1976. The following list comprises the most significant of those guidelines, in chronological order. Following each entry is a citation to the report or other publication in which the guidelines originally appeared.

> *Agreement on Guidelines for Classroom Copying in Not-for-Profit Educational Institutions with Respect to Books and Periodicals*, March 1976. (U.S. Congress. House. *Copyright Law Revision*, 94th Cong., 2d sess. [1976]. H. Doc. 1476: 68–70.)
>
> *Guidelines for Educational Uses of Music*, April 1976. (U.S. Congress. House. *Copyright Law Revision*, 94th Cong., 2d sess. [1976]. H. Doc. 1476: 70–71.)
>
> *Guidelines for Off-Air Recording of Broadcast Programming for Educational Purposes*, October 1981. (U.S. Congress. *Congressional Record*, vol. 127, no. 18, pp. 24,048–49 [1981]. Reprinted soon after at U.S. Congress. House. *Report on Piracy and Counterfeiting Amendments*, 97th Cong., 1st sess. [1982]. H. Doc. 495: 8–9.)
>
> *Model Policy concerning College and University Photocopying for Classroom, Research and Library Reserve Use*, American Library Association, March 1982. (Originally published as a separate pamphlet from the American Library Association. Available at http://www.cni.org/docs/infopols/ALA.html [scroll down the page to find the right item]).
>
> *Library and Classroom Use of Copyrighted Videotapes and Computer Software*, American Library Association, February 1986. (Mary Hutchings Reed and Debra Stanek, "Library and Classroom Use of Copyrighted Videotapes and Computer Software," *American Libraries* 17 [February 1986]: supp., pp. A–D. Available at http://www.ifla.org/documents/infopol/copyright/ala-1.txt.)
>
> *Using Software: A Guide to the Ethical and Legal Use of Software for Members of the Academic Community*, Educom, January 1992. (Originally published as a separate pamphlet from Educom, a predecessor organization to Educause. Available at http://www.ifla.org/documents/infopol/copyright/educom.txt.)
>
> *Fair-Use Guidelines for Electronic Reserve Systems*, March 1996. (Originally developed by participants in CONFU but not included in the final report. Available at http://www.mville.edu/Administration/staff/Jeff_Rosedale/guidelines.htm.)

> The CONFU final report includes the original publication of three guidelines on issues of digital images, distance learning, and educational multimedia. That report is available at http://www.uspto.gov/web/offices/dcom/olia/confu/confurep.pdf. The Conference on Fair Use was conducted under the oversight of the U.S. Patent and Trademark Office and was rooted in a 1995 report on the National Information Infrastructure: http://www.uspto.gov/web/offices/com/doc/ipnii/index.html.

Proposal for Educational Fair Use Guidelines for Digital Images, Conference on Fair Use, November 1998. (Information Infrastructure Task Force, Working Group on Intellectual Property Rights, *Conference on Fair Use: Final Report to the Commissioner on the Conclusion of the Conference on Fair Use*, November 1998, 33–41.)

Proposal for Educational Fair Use Guidelines for Distance Learning, Conference on Fair Use, November 1998. (Information Infrastructure Task Force, Working Group on Intellectual Property Rights, *Conference on Fair Use: Final Report to the Commissioner on the Conclusion of the Conference on Fair Use*, November 1998, 43–48.)

Proposal for Fair Use Guidelines for Educational Multimedia, Conference on Fair Use, November 1998. (Information Infrastructure Task Force, Working Group on Intellectual Property Rights, *Conference on Fair Use: Final Report to the Commissioner on the Conclusion of the Conference on Fair Use*, November 1998, 49–59.)

> These guidelines are reprinted in a host of different books and other publications. Many of them, especially the earliest guidelines, are available on the website of the Music Library Association at http://www.lib.jmu.edu/org/ mla/Guidelines/.

> Yet another set of copyright guidelines focuses on making copies for interlibrary loans. These guidelines are not about fair use, but instead are an interpretation of a provision of Section 108. They are examined in chapter 12.

Some guidelines have proven to be enormously influential on our conceptualization of fair use. The earliest document, on photocopying for classroom purposes, reinterprets the four factors into such notions as "spontaneous" copying, and it calls on teachers to meticulously count words on the page before making multiple copies of articles as handouts. These standards have appeared often in the literature of the law and in policy documents at colleges, universities, schools, and other institutions throughout the country. However influential the guidelines may be, their role has been a mixed blessing. For many users, guidelines are a source of certainty when fair use seems unsettled. For many other users, guidelines are a constraint on the law's flexibility.

The Example of Electronic Reserves

Among the guidelines listed above is a document from 1996 that attempts to articulate the meaning of fair use for electronic reserve systems. In some respects, these systems might be seen as a variation on the library service of making and delivering copies of items. Section 108 of the Copyright Act, as detailed in chapter 12 of this book, allows such copying. But Section 108 is generally limited to single copies, and it does not apply to delivery systems that involve multiple users and multiple copies.

One might wonder if allowing students to access materials from outside the library building might be a form of distance learning. The TEACH Act, summarized in chapter 11, offers new terms on which educational institutions can copy and transmit copyrighted materials to students. E-reserves systems typically include copies of articles and book chapters that students access from campus or from afar in connection with course requirements. But the TEACH Act allows such "displays" only in an amount comparable to that which would be used in the classroom. In other words, if students would conventionally read the assigned text outside the classroom, the TEACH Act does not allow it in distance education.

Once again, we are faced with a common situation in the law. None of the specific statutory exceptions covers our particular needs. We may consequently turn to fair use. Across the country, different libraries, publishers, and copyright experts have reached widely differing conclusions about the meaning of fair use for electronic reserves. These issues were a priority during the CONFU proceedings. A subgroup of CONFU, including the present author, drafted the 1996 guidelines mentioned above. Due to a sharply divided membership, however, the final report did not include the guidelines.

What does the absence of guidelines on e-reserves mean? The lack of formal guidelines can be a blessing. Libraries should return to the four factors of fair use. Some of the scenarios in chapter 9, particularly as related to classroom copies and coursepacks, suggest much about the meaning of the factors as applied to copies of articles and chapters and other works that are digitized and delivered to students on library systems.

> Jeff Rosedale of Manhattanville College Library has prepared the Electronic Reserves Clearinghouse. His valuable website has links to systems, policies, and information from numerous libraries and other organizations on the subject of electronic reserves. See http://www.mville.edu/Administration/staff/ Jeff_Rosedale/.

The lack of guidelines on e-reserves actually opens new possibilities for librarians to implement their own policies or procedures. Libraries might explore password restrictions on access, limit copies to only brief excerpts, or perhaps allow only works that are already in the library collections. Libraries can design other limits into the system, tying those parameters to the statutory factors, in order to create local "guidelines." In fact, that is exactly what libraries have done. The standards of fair use for e-reserves vary greatly across the country. As a result, we are able to experiment with possibilities and to learn from one another's efforts.

What to Do with the Guidelines?

For many other common needs, we do have guidelines that attempt to define fair use. The main motivation behind most of the guidelines has been to bring some degree of certainty to common fair-use applications. Yet none of these guidelines has any force of law. None of them has been enacted into law by Congress, and none has been adopted as a binding standard of fair use in any court decision. So do they present appropriate "answers" to some fair-use problems?

Whatever the possible benefits of guidelines, the author of this book has written at length about their shortcomings. Among the deficiencies:

- They often misinterpret fair use, infusing it with variables and conditions that are not part of the law.
- They create rigidity in the application of fair use, sacrificing the flexibility that allows fair use to have meaning for new needs, technologies, and materials.
- They tend to espouse the narrowest interpretations of the law in order to gain support from diverse groups.

Whatever the virtues or hazards of the guidelines, each individual or organization must decide whether to adopt or follow any of them. Even the most enthusiastic supporter of the guidelines, however, cannot avoid some of their consequences. The guidelines will never address all needs; we will steadily turn to the factors in the law to understand each new situation. The guidelines also demand diligent oversight and enforcement if they really are to become policy standards for educators, librarians, and others. For example, if the guidelines on classroom photocopying are the limits of fair use, then the educational institution will need to expect compliance with the full roster of detailed conditions in them. Implementing standards from the guidelines is often more demanding than struggling with the flexibility of fair use.

Basing a decision on the four factors in the statute, rather than on guidelines, can have real advantages. The law's flexibility is important for enabling fair use to meet future needs and to promote progress in the academic setting or elsewhere. Relying on fair use also creates some important protections for educators and librarians. The good-faith application of fair use can lead a court to cut some of the most serious liabilities that educators or librarians might face in an infringement lawsuit. The only way to apply fair use in "good faith" is by learning the law and applying it; the only way to apply the law is by working with the four factors in the statute. In the final analysis, the law itself may offer greater security than can the "certainty" of the fair-use guidelines.

> Chapter 13 includes more details about the liabilities that can arise in a copyright infringement lawsuit, as well as the reduction of liabilities in the event of a good-faith application of fair use.

PART IV ■ Focus on Education and Libraries

11

Distance Education and the TEACH Act

KEY POINTS

- ◼ The TEACH Act allows uses of copyrighted works in distance learning.

- ◼ Implementing the new law requires policies, technological controls, and compliance with many other conditions.

- ◼ Not all copyrighted works can be used in full under the TEACH Act.

- ◼ Fair use continues to be an important means for lawful use of works in distance education.

The rapid expansion of distance education in recent years has accelerated the use of copyrighted materials on the Internet and in other networked systems. That growth also has led to a proliferation of copyright questions among educators and librarians. Possibilities of infringement arise whenever text, images, sounds, and other works are scanned, uploaded, transmitted, and stored or copied by students enrolled in online courses. The TEACH Act, enacted by Congress and signed into law in late 2002, creates a new exception to the rights of owners by allowing educators to use protected works in distance education without risk of infringement.[1]

Good News and Bad News

The TEACH Act, or more formally the Technology, Education and Copyright Harmonization Act, offers benefits along with limits and responsibilities. As long as educators remain within the boundaries of the law, they can avoid infringements and need not seek permission from, or pay royalties to, the copyright owner. These benefits, however, are not easy to secure. Indeed, complying with

---

This chapter is based in part on Kenneth D. Crews, "Copyright and Distance Education: Making Sense of the TEACH Act," *Change* 35 (November–December 2003): 34–39.

the TEACH Act means satisfying a rather lengthy list of conditions in the statute. Even then, the TEACH Act still places limitations on the use of many copyrighted works. If instructors and their educational institutions are to reap the law's benefits, they must take careful steps to implement it.

> The TEACH Act is codified at Section 110(2) of the Copyright Act. It replaced the original Section 110(2) that had been part of the law since 1978, but the prior law had limits and constraints that made it generally unworkable for web-based courses.

This balance of rights and limits reveals the tension between copyright owners and users. Authors and publishers of textbooks, producers of films, composers of music, and other copyright owners often want maximum protection for their work and the ability to generate all possible revenue from it. For many of these owners, educators are their main users and a source of potential revenue. By contrast, teachers preparing new online courses might want liberal rights of use, especially if the purpose is for nonprofit education. The TEACH Act is a compromise between maximum protection and liberal rights of use. It allows some uses in distance education, but not all.

The statute is also built around a particular vision of distance education that generally involves performances and displays of works in a manner much like a classroom experience. The TEACH Act permits uses of copyrighted works in the context of "mediated instructional activities" that are akin in many respects to the conduct of traditional instructional sessions.[2] For example, the law anticipates that students will sometimes access materials only within a roughly prescribed time period and may not necessarily store or review them later in the academic term.[3]

Similarly, faculty members will be able to include copyrighted materials, but often only in portions or under conditions analogous to conventional teaching. Stated more bluntly, this law is generally not intended to permit scanning and uploading of any lengthy work to a website for unlimited access.

The TEACH Act also suggests another development: no one person acting alone is able to comply with the law. The law requires the adoption of institutional copyright policies, the distribution of information to the educational community concerning copyright, the implementation of technological controls, and adherence to the "portion" limits of allowable materials.[4] In the past, compliance with copyright law had typically been the responsibility of each instructor. Under the TEACH Act, however, the educational institution itself will likely have to participate actively in the compliance effort.

Requirements of the TEACH Act

Unlike the relatively broad and flexible terms of fair use, the limitations in the TEACH Act are highly detailed and are generally exacting in their definition of allowed uses of copyrighted works. A close reading of the statute reveals a roster of requirements which can be usefully grouped into three categories: institutional and policy requirements, technology requirements, and instructional planning requirements. Keep in mind that the benefits of the law can apply only upon meeting all of the prescribed requirements.

Institutional and Policy Requirements

The TEACH Act mandates various policies, information resources, and notifications about copyright.[5] These requirements likely involve institutional decision making. They can demand careful interpretation of the law and may have implications beyond online courses. Therefore, meeting these requirements will likely fall within the realm of deans, directors, legal counsel, or other central administrators.

Accredited institutions. The TEACH Act applies only to a "governmental body or an accredited nonprofit educational institution."[6] In general, colleges and universities accredited by a recognized agency, or elementary and secondary schools recognized under state law, will easily qualify. Programs offered by federal, state, or local government agencies, including public libraries, may also qualify. The application of the TEACH Act to government bodies can be broad, ranging from professional enrichment courses offered by local governments to the full curricula of military academies.

What organizations cannot use the TEACH Act? The law will not benefit unaccredited start-ups, some trade schools, and various for-profit institutions.

Copyright policy. The new law requires educational institutions to institute "policies regarding copyright."[7] Although the statute does not offer many details, one can surmise that such policies should specify standards for incorporating copyrighted works into distance education. Whatever the form or content, policymaking usually requires deliberate and concerted action by proper authorities within the educational institution.

Policy development can be a complicated process, involving lengthy deliberations and multiple levels of review and approval. Formal policymaking may be preferable, but informal procedural standards that effectively guide relevant activities may well satisfy the TEACH Act requirement.

Copyright information. The institution must provide "informational materials" regarding copyright.[8] In this instance, the language specifies that the materials must "accurately describe, and promote compliance with, the laws of the United States relating to copyright." These materials must be provided to "faculty, students, and relevant staff members." Institutions might consider developing websites, distributing printed materials, or providing information through the distance-education program itself.

Many educational institutions are developing copyright information resources to help instructors and others. The rich trove of information readily available on the Internet and in publication means that we can borrow and learn from one another. Creating a website with links to these available materials can ease the way toward satisfying this requirement.

Notice to students. The statute further specifies that the institution must provide "notice to students that materials used in connection with the course may be subject to copyright protection."[9] This "notice" may be a brief statement simply alerting students to copyright implications. The notice could be included on distribution materials in the class or perhaps on an opening frame of the distance-education course or in a "pop-up" box on the course website.

Technology Requirements

New technologies may be driving much of the growth of distance education and the potential for copyright infringements. The TEACH Act accordingly calls upon technological innovation to inhibit the abuse of copyrighted materials. The law requires institutions to implement a variety of technological methods for controlling access to, and limiting the further dissemination of, copyrighted works.

Limited access to enrolled students. The new law calls upon the institution to limit transmissions to students enrolled in the particular course "to the extent technologically feasible."[10] This requirement to limit access should not be difficult to satisfy. Most educational institutions have course management systems or other tools that can use passwords or other restrictions on access.

Technological controls on retention and further dissemination. The TEACH Act applies to a wide variety of means for delivery of distance education, but a few provisions apply only in the case of "digital transmissions." In such instances, the institution must apply technical measures to prevent "retention of the work in accessible form by recipients of the transmission . . . for longer than the class session."[11] The statute offers no explicit definition of a "class session," but language in congressional reports suggests that any digital transmissions of works in a retainable format would be confined to a finite time, after which students would be unable to access it.

> This undefined notion of a "class session" is one of the most perplexing aspects of the TEACH Act. From the educator's viewpoint, constraining the use to a limited span of time seems to defeat one of the leading benefits of distance education: that students can work with materials at their own pace and return to earlier readings for reinforcement. This limit in the TEACH Act may not be terribly onerous. The law is a restriction on the length of time that the "recipient" or student can retain the electronic item; this provision may not directly bar retention of the work on the institution's server for repeated access by students.

Technological controls on dissemination. Also in the case of "digital transmissions," the institution must apply "technological measures" to prevent students from engaging in "unauthorized further dissemination of the work in accessible form."

The technological controls to prevent students from retaining and disseminating the work need not be airtight. The TEACH Act specifies that the technology must "reasonably prevent" the activity. The technology might not be perfect, and a student might find a way around it, but at least the institution should use its best effort and stay informed about the latest possibilities.

Technological Complications

These restrictions on the accessing, copying, and further sharing of materials address serious concerns from copyright owners. On the other hand, many technology experts question whether the implementation of *effective* technological measures is even possible. Once content reaches the student's computer, blocking all means of downloading or copying the materials may be impossible. Once materials are stored, little can restrict further duplication and distribution of them. The U.S. Patent and Trademark Office has collected information about effective technological restrictions for further study.[12] Educational institutions will need to continue to find the best available means—even if imperfect—for complying with the law.

> The steady expansion of technological innovation will always raise more possibilities for complying with the TEACH Act. Conversely, as time passes, today's technological measures may no longer meet the requirements of the TEACH Act if students acquire the ability to bypass a protective measure.

Various other technological requirements appear in the law. For example, if the copyrighted content has restrictive codes or other embedded "management systems" to regulate storage or dissemination of the work, the institution may not "engage in conduct that could reasonably be expected to interfere with [such] technological measures."[13]

The TEACH Act also explicitly exonerates educational institutions from liability that may result from most instances of "transient or temporary storage of material."[14] Furthermore, the TEACH Act amended Section 112 of the Copyright Act, addressing the issue of "ephemeral recordings."[15] The new Section 112(f)(1) explicitly allows educational institutions to retain copies of their digital transmissions that include copyrighted materials used pursuant to the new law. All of these provisions of the law create new responsibilities that will most assuredly become the domain of technology experts at educational institutions.

Instructional Requirements

In addition to the many conditions about access, technology, and policy, the TEACH Act further defines limits on the selection of substantive instructional content. Most decisions about course content are usually left to instructors, in part because of traditions of academic freedom, but also because they know their subjects best. Instructors will therefore be instrumental in complying with the law as they make crucial decisions about the selection and quantity of materials to incorporate into distance-learning courses.

> Chapter 5 examines the rights of copyright owners and explains the concepts of "displays" and "performances." Displays are generally static images, whether of artwork, text, photographs, or other works; performances generally occur with the playing of music or audiovisual works and the recital of text, poetry, or plays. Distance education, as well as classroom instruction, routinely includes many displays and performances.

The limits in the TEACH Act are best understood by comparison to previous law, which drew sharp distinctions between allowed and disallowed works. These distinctions were built upon the statutory concepts of "displays" and "performances." Previous law allowed "displays" of any type of work, but allowed "performances" of only "nondramatic literary works" and "nondramatic musical works." Consequently, many dramatic works were excluded from distance education, as were performances of audiovisual materials and sound recordings. Such narrowly crafted exceptions were problematic at best. The TEACH Act expands upon previous law in several important respects.

Works explicitly allowed. The new law now explicitly permits:

- Performances of nondramatic literary works
- Performances of nondramatic musical works
- Performances of any other work, including dramatic works and audiovisual works, but only in "reasonable and limited portions"
- Displays of any work "in an amount comparable to that which is typically displayed in the course of a live classroom session"[16]

Works explicitly excluded. A few categories of works are specifically left outside the range of permitted materials under the TEACH Act:

- Works that are marketed "primarily for performance or display as part of mediated instructional activities transmitted via digital networks." For example, materials available through online databases, or marketed and delivered for educational uses through "digital" systems, may be outside of the TEACH Act. The law generally steers users to those sources directly, rather than allowing educators to digitize and deliver their own copies of them.
- Performances or displays given by means of copies "not lawfully made and acquired" under the U.S. Copyright Act, if the educational institution "knew or had reason to believe" that they were not lawfully made and acquired.[17]

Instructor oversight. The statute mandates the instructor's participation in the planning and conduct of the distance-education program as transmitted. An instructor seeking to use materials under the protection of the new statute must adhere to the following requirements:

- The performance or display must be "made by, at the direction of, or under the actual supervision of an instructor."

- The materials are transmitted "as an integral part of a class session offered as a regular part of the systematic, mediated instructional activities" of the educational institution.
- The copyrighted materials are "directly related and of material assistance to the teaching content of the transmission."[18]

These three requirements share some common objectives: to assure that the instructor ultimately supervises the uses of copyrighted works, and that the materials serve educational pursuits and are not for entertainment or other purposes.

> What are "mediated instructional activities"? This language means that the uses of materials in the program must be "analogous to the type of performance or display that would take place in a live classroom setting." "Mediated instructional activities" also does not encompass uses of textbooks and other materials "which are typically purchased or acquired by the students." *U.S. Copyright Act*, 17 *U.S.C.* § 110(2) (2005). The statute again seems to be making a fundamental point: if students would ordinarily buy and keep the materials, that content should not be scanned and uploaded as part of distance education.

Converting Analog to Digital

Troublesome to many copyright owners was the prospect that their analog materials would be converted to digital formats, and hence made susceptible to easy downloading and dissemination. The TEACH Act takes a cautious approach and allows conversions only in quantities allowed for performance and display in the course, and only if a digital version of the work is not "available to the institution."[19]

As a practical matter, educators again need to make decisions in the context of specific limits of the law, and they may need to investigate whether the work exists in digital format before scanning and digitizing anew.

Making Plans and Looking Ahead

The TEACH Act holds out the prospect of allowing a considerable range of copyrighted works in distance education, but only after meeting the rather significant burden of compliance. Perhaps the most significant aspect of compliance is that no one person is likely able to meet the challenge alone. Multiple parties within the college or university will need to participate; central administrators and policymakers will have a role of growing importance; technology experts will need to implement systems and controls; and instructors must develop courses with attention to limits on the types and quantity of allowable materials.

> Perhaps the first step in implementing the TEACH Act is to assemble a team of leaders and experts. The first question might be: are we willing and able to do the work? If the group is not motivated to make the law work, it simply may not be right for your institution. After all, the TEACH Act is not mandatory. You may instead rely on fair use or permissions.

> Fair use has long applied to distance education. As noted above, the earlier version of Section 110(2) was supposed to cover distance education, but the law failed to have meaning in the online setting. Realistically, educators therefore have depended for years on fair use to cover uses in all forms of distance-education courses. Fair use remains a legally valid alternative when the TEACH Act does not work. Chapters 7 through 10 examine fair use in considerable detail.

Because the TEACH Act has limits, many uses of copyrighted works that may be desirable or essential for effective teaching may simply be outside the scope of the act. In anticipation of those limits, educators should also be prepared to explore alternatives. Some possibilities are:

- Employing alternative methods for delivering materials to students, including the expansion of innovative library services and access to databases and retrieval systems
- Applying the law of fair use, which may allow uses beyond those detailed in the TEACH Act
- Securing permission from copyright owners for uses not sanctioned by TEACH, fair use, or other provision of the law. Chapter 17 of this book includes guidance for seeking permissions.

The TEACH Act is a relatively new law, but in its few years of existence it apparently has gained only modest acceptance. The principal reason may be simply that the law is too complicated for casual compliance, and its conditions may appear confusing, foreboding, or perhaps impossible. The TEACH Act may find its greatest potential when applied to courses that are initiated and overseen by a centralized office. Someone with oversight authority may have the best opportunity to make sure that the litany of legal details is addressed, and that the policymakers and technology specialists are enlisted to offer their skills and services.

By contrast, the individual instructor who is scanning and uploading materials to a website may not have the resources, talents, or even the inclination to address every provision of the TEACH Act. An individual instructor is typically not well positioned to evaluate the detailed law and to make judgments about legal interpretations, choices, and compliance. Until some level of centralized authority at an educational institution takes the lead, the TEACH Act will probably not be a realistic option, but instructors have the continuing opportunity of turning to fair use and other constructive options.

Notes

1. *Technology, Education and Copyright Harmonization Act*, Public Law 107-273, *U.S. Statutes at Large* 116 (2002): 1910, codified at 17 *U.S.C.* §§ 110(2), 112(f) (2005).
2. *U.S. Copyright Act*, 17 *U.S.C.* § 110(2) (2005).
3. *U.S. Copyright Act*, 17 *U.S.C.* § 110(2).
4. *U.S. Copyright Act*, 17 *U.S.C.* § 110(2)(D) (2005).
5. *U.S. Copyright Act*, 17 *U.S.C.* § 110(2)(D).
6. *U.S. Copyright Act*, 17 *U.S.C.* § 110(2).
7. *U.S. Copyright Act*, 17 *U.S.C.* § 110(2)(D).
8. *U.S. Copyright Act*, 17 *U.S.C.* § 110(2)(D).
9. *U.S. Copyright Act*, 17 *U.S.C.* § 110(2)(D).
10. *U.S. Copyright Act*, 17 *U.S.C.* § 110(2)(C) (2005).
11. *U.S. Copyright Act*, 17 *U.S.C.* § 110(2)(D)(ii) (2005).
12. For the text of a 2003 report, see http://www.uspto.gov/web/offices/dcom/olia/teachreport.pdf.
13. *U.S. Copyright Act*, 17 *U.S.C.* § 110(2)(D)(ii)(II) (2005).
14. *U.S. Copyright Act*, 17 *U.S.C.* § 110(2) (2005).
15. *U.S. Copyright Act*, 17 *U.S.C.* § 112(f) (2005).
16. *U.S. Copyright Act*, 17 *U.S.C.* § 110(2).
17. *U.S. Copyright Act*, 17 *U.S.C.* § 110(2).
18. *U.S. Copyright Act*, 17 *U.S.C.* § 110(2)(A–C) (2005).
19. *U.S. Copyright Act*, 17 *U.S.C.* § 112(f)(2) (2005).

12

Libraries and the Special Provisions of Section 108

KEY POINTS

■ Section 108 allows many libraries to make copies of materials for preservation, private study, and interlibrary loan.

■ The opportunities under Section 108 do not extend equally to all types of works.

■ Section 108 requires compliance with various requirements, but most libraries should be able to meet them and enjoy the benefits of the law.

American copyright law includes numerous specific provisions limiting the rights of copyright owners, including a provision specifically applicable to libraries. Section 108 of the Copyright Act allows libraries to make and distribute copies of materials for specified purposes under specified conditions. Although meticulous, it can offer important support for library services.[1]

Section 108 allows libraries, within limits, to make copies of many works for the following three purposes: copies for the preservation of library collections; copies for private study by users; and copies to send pursuant to interlibrary loan (ILL) arrangements. Once it has determined that the copying is for one of those purposes, the library must then resolve these questions:

■ Is the library eligible to enjoy the benefits of the law?
■ Is the copyrighted work one of the types of works that may be used pursuant to this statute?
■ Has the library adhered to the conditions for making copies for each of the allowed purposes?

Eligibility Requirements of Section 108

Before a library can have the benefits of Section 108, it must comply with certain general requirements and limits. Most academic and public libraries will have little trouble meeting these requirements. The statute establishes the following "ground rules" for using Section 108:

> What libraries will not qualify to use Section 108? Private libraries, corporate libraries, and other libraries that are closed to outside users may be outside Section 108. But the exclusion is not sweeping. A library qualifies if it is open to outside users "doing research in a specialized field." In other words, if a specialized corporate library admits outside researchers, even selectively, that library may qualify.

- The library must be open to the public or to outside researchers. Nearly every public and academic library will meet this standard.
- The copying must be made "without any purpose of direct or indirect commercial advantage." This requirement may exclude copies that are made by a public library, but that are for a commercial document-delivery service. It may also mean that a corporate library may be eligible to use this law, if the copies themselves are not specifically for commercial uses.
- The library may make only single copies on "isolated and unrelated" occasions and may not under most circumstances make multiple copies or engage in "systematic reproduction or distribution of single or multiple copies."[2]

> Although Section 108 generally permits only single copies, the provisions that apply to preservation copies allow up to three copies of a single work. This chapter details the preservation requirements.

- Each copy made must include a notice of copyright.

Since the passage of Section 108 in 1976, libraries and publishers have debated whether the "notice" on the copy must be the formal copyright notice found on the original (such as the notice near the beginning of this book) or some general indication that copyright law may apply (such as "use of this material is governed by copyright law").

The Digital Millennium Copyright Act, enacted in late 1998, resolved this dilemma.[3] All copies made under Section 108 must now include the copyright notice as it appears on the original. If no notice appears on the original, then the copy must only include "a legend stating that the work may be protected by copyright."

Works That May Be Copied

Section 108 sets specific limits on the types of materials that libraries may copy. The types of materials vary, depending on whether the copies are for preservation or private study. If the library is making the copies for a patron's private study or for sending in interlibrary loan, copies of the following materials are *not* allowed:

- Musical works
- Pictorial, graphic, or sculptural works
- Motion pictures or audiovisual works

> Be careful to distinguish between "musical works" and "sound recordings." Under copyright law, these are two different types of works. A "musical work" is the musical composition. A musical work can be in the form of a printed score or a recording of a performance. Under Section 108, copying a sound recording of music may not be permitted. But a "sound recording" of spoken words is a version of a literary work. Copying that recording may be allowed under Section 108. Chapter 14 gives much more insight into issues of music and sound recordings.

The law then allows libraries to make copies of a wide range of other materials in accordance with Section 108:

- Other types of works that are not specifically excluded by the preceding list. Such works may include the contents of journals, newspapers, books, and other textual works, regardless of whether they are in analog or digital formats. The scope of allowed works could also extend to computer software, sound recordings, dance notations, and a wide range of copyrightable materials.
- Audiovisual works "dealing with news."
- Pictures and graphics "published as illustrations, diagrams, or similar adjuncts" to works that may otherwise be copied. In other words, if you can copy the article, you can also copy the picture or chart that is in the article.

By contrast, if the copies are made for the preservation of library materials, the scope of materials is not limited. Thus, for example, while most audiovisual works may not be reproduced for a patron's study, they may be reproduced for preservation.

Copies for Preservation

Once the library is qualified to use Section 108, and proper materials are identified, the library must next meet the various conditions for each use. Under what conditions may the library make copies for preservation?

If the work is unpublished, preservation copies are permitted upon meeting both of these conditions:

- The work is currently in the collection of the library making the copy.
- The copies are solely for preservation or security, or for deposit at another library. The library can therefore make a copy of a manuscript for patron use, and store the original for safekeeping. The library that owns the original may also make a copy and contribute the copy to the collections of another library. The library receiving the copied work must also be eligible under the terms of Section 108.

If the work was previously published, preservation copies are permitted upon meeting both of these conditions:

- The copies are solely for replacement of works that are damaged, deteriorating, lost or stolen, or if the format of a work has become obsolete.
- The library conducts a reasonable investigation to conclude that an unused replacement cannot be obtained at a fair price.

> What is an "obsolete" format? The statute defines the notion to mean that the machine or device necessary for that format "is no longer manufactured or is no longer reasonably available in the commercial marketplace." In other words, if you cannot find newly made or sold players, you may be able to make preservation copies of your collection of eight-track disco music.

The Digital Millennium Copyright Act also clarified the rights of a library to make preservation copies in a digital medium. Digital preservation copies may be made of both published and unpublished works under all the conditions set forth above. In addition, "any such copy or phonorecord that is reproduced in digital format" may not be "made available to the public in that format outside the premises of the library or archives." To oversimplify, machine-readable digital formats must generally be confined to the library building.

> Why did Congress confine the digital copies to the premises of the library? The principal reason lies in the nature of digital media and networked systems. If a library could make a preservation copy and upload it to a server for wide accessibility, the library would be acting very much like a publisher of that work. The current limit in the law may be too restrictive, but it is a reminder that copyright owners are concerned about the possible competitive effects of some library services.

Copies for Private Study

Under what conditions may the library make copies for library users to study and keep? Here the law sets two basic standards. One standard applies to copies of articles, book chapters, or other short works. A slightly more demanding standard applies to copies of entire books and other such works.

If the copy is of an article, book chapter, or other short work, these conditions apply:

- The copy becomes the property of the user.
- The library has no notice that the copy is for any purpose other than private study, scholarship, or research.
- The library displays a warning notice where orders for copies are accepted and on order forms.

> Does the library have to actually know that the copy is for private study and not for a business or other purpose? No. The librarian taking the order for the copy is probably best to know nothing about the purpose of the use. Once the librarian has reason to know that the copy is for some purpose other than private study, the library's copying under Section 108 may need to end.

If the copy is of an entire book or other work, or of a substantial part of such a work, these conditions apply:

- The library conducts a reasonable investigation to conclude that a copy cannot be obtained at a fair price.
- The copy becomes the property of the user.
- The library has no notice that the copy is for any purpose other than private study, scholarship, or research.
- The library displays a warning notice where orders for copies are accepted and on order forms.

> The notice on order forms is usually a simple warning statement about copyright protection. By contrast, the notice that libraries must display at the place where orders are received is detailed in regulations issued by the U.S. Copyright Office. See *Code of Federal Regulations*, title 37, vol. 1, sec. 201.14 (2005).

Copies for Interlibrary Loan

Section 108 also allows libraries to make copies and to receive copies of materials in the name of interlibrary loan services. For the library that is making and sending the copies, the rule for ILL is fairly straightforward. In general, the copy must be made pursuant to the standards already detailed in this chapter. The copies requested through ILL are generally articles, chapters, and other short works that are copied for purposes of private study and research. Section 108 outlines the circumstances when a library may make such copies, whether the end user is present at the library or is making the request through ILL.

The rules for the library receiving the copy, however, are a little different. That library must adhere to this standard: the interlibrary arrangements cannot have, as their purpose or effect, that the library receiving the copies on behalf of requesting patrons "does so in such aggregate quantities as to substitute for a subscription to or purchase of such work." The point of this language is to remind libraries that when the demand for a journal or other work reaches a sufficient amount, the library ought to consider buying its own instead of relying on ILL. The problem, of course, is that the law does not specifically define the limit.

To help clarify the limit on a library's ability to receive copies, Congress established the National Commission on New Technological Uses of Copyrighted Works (CONTU) shortly after enacting Section 108. CONTU issued its final report in 1979, and proposed guidelines that bring specificity to the quantity limits of the law. The CONTU standards generally allow a library, during one calendar year, to receive up to five copies of articles from the most recent five years of a journal title.

> The CONTU guidelines are hardly complete. They encompass only copies of recent journal articles. Libraries are left to their own good judgment about the limits of the law as applied to older materials, book chapters, and other works. For the full text of the CONTU final report, see http://digital-law-online.info/CONTU/contu1.html.

After reaching that quota, the general expectation is that the receiving library will evaluate its alternatives. The library may purchase its own subscription to the journal. Some libraries simply choose not to fulfill requests for additional articles from that journal, a strategy that leaves the next user completely unserved. Many libraries instead seek permission from the copyright owner, or they pay a fee to the Copyright Clearance Center for a license to make the additional copies. Other libraries might more directly reconsider the appropriateness of the CONTU guidelines. These standards are not the law, and libraries have the ability to evaluate whether some other interpretation of Section 108 may be appropriate.

Copier Machines in the Library

Section 108 has one more provision that is routinely important to libraries. Section 108(f)(1) gives libraries protection from infringements that a visitor may commit when using unsupervised copier machines in the library. As long as the library displays a notice informing users that making copies may be subject to copyright law, the statute can release the library and its staff from liability. The user of the machine is still responsible for any infringements.

> A form of notice commonly posted on "reproducing equipment" in libraries states: "Notice: The copyright law of the United States (Title 17, U.S. Code) governs the making of photocopies or other reproductions of copyrighted material. The person using this equipment is liable for any infringement."

This provision of the statute offers protection to libraries that post notices on unsupervised "reproducing equipment" at the library. The provision does not narrowly refer to "photocopy machines." The benefit to libraries could be considerable, and the cost of compliance is negligible. A library is well advised to post a notice on all unsupervised photocopy machines, as well as on VCRs, tape decks, microfilm readers, computers, printers, and any other equipment that is capable of making copies.

Notes

1. *U.S. Copyright Act*, 17 *U.S.C.* § 108 (2005).
2. *U.S. Copyright Act*, 17 *U.S.C.* § 108(g) (2005).
3. *Digital Millennium Copyright Act*, Public Law 105-304, *U.S. Statutes at Large* 112 (1998): 2860.

Responsibilities, Liabilities, and Doing the Right Thing

KEY POINTS

■ An infringer of copyright can face extensive liabilities.

■ Educators and librarians who exercise fair use in "good faith" may avoid some of the most significant liability risks.

■ New law offers a "safe harbor" for online service providers.

■ State universities and other state agencies may be protected under "sovereign immunity."

So far, this book has generally avoided the topic of liability for copyright infringement. This sidestepping of liability is no accident. The fundamental objective of this book is to educate readers and prepare them to handle copyright situations in an informed and good-faith manner, thus helping to avoid liability.

Yet the time may come when you might have infringed the rights of a copyright owner. For example, you "reproduced" a protected work without permission and in a manner that is not within fair use or another exception. You may in another situation be on the other side of the scenario; perhaps you are the copyright owner, asserting a claim against a purported infringer.

What Are the Legal Risks?

What is at stake in an infringement action? In the unlikely event of a court's finding that you have committed an infringement, the consequences can be staggering. An injunction can bar further unlawful uses; the court can impound the copies and your equipment; and you can be ordered to reimburse losses that the copyright owner incurred or pay the profits you gained from the wrongdoing.[1]

The copyright owner who successfully makes an infringement claim may also be entitled to receive two other remedies that involve significant dollars. First, the owner can seek "statutory damages" of up to $30,000 per work infringed, in lieu of actual damages or profits.[2] Second, the owner may also ask for reimbursement of attorney fees and the costs of bringing the litigation.[3] These amounts are not to be underestimated. Recall the case of *Basic Books, Inc. v. Kinko's Graphics Corp.* from chapter 9.[4] The court ruled that Kinko's had infringed the copyrights and ordered it to pay $510,000 in statutory damages. Kinko's also had to pay the publishers' attorney fees and costs, in the total amount of $1,395,000.[5]

The dollar amounts may be overwhelming, but statutory damages and attorney fees are generally available to the copyright owner only if the owner registered the work with the U.S. Copyright Office before the infringement occurred.[6] Recall from chapter 3 that registration and other formalities are no longer required. You may well be the copyright owner without registering the work, and you may still be able to win your case and obtain damages and other remedies. But only after timely registration are you entitled to what are often the most lucrative remedies in an infringement case—statutory damages and attorney fees. The lesson to copyright owners is clear: if you are serious about protecting your copyrights, you ought to consider registering the claim. Moreover, you should register early before any infringement has occurred.

> To be eligible for statutory damages and attorney fees, the work generally must have been registered before the infringement occurred. In the case of a published work, the Copyright Act allows a grace period of three months after first publication to make the registration. *U.S. Copyright Act*, 17 *U.S.C.* § 412(2) (2005). Registration can occur long after publication, but the owner will only qualify for the added rights with respect to infringements occurring after the registration date.

If the infringement is "willful," the consequences skyrocket. The statutory damages can jump from $30,000 to $150,000 per work infringed. Criminal liability may also apply to willful copying, and Congress has recently toughened criminal liabilities, applying the penalties more explicitly to infringements by electronic means.[7] (Generally, an infringement is "willful" if the user knew or had reason to know that the actions were unlawful.)

Good Faith and Good News

With a variety of potential legal liabilities hanging over our heads, how can librarians, educators, and others reasonably live amidst the uncertainty that copyright sometimes brings? Fortunately, the Copyright Act offers some important protection in response to exactly this realistic need. The law calls on each of us to act in an informed and good-faith manner.

This basic advice may seem trivial, but it is actually of central importance, particularly for educators and librarians working with fair use. Reasonable people can and will disagree about the meaning of fair use. Congress recognized that it was enacting a law open to significant differences of interpretation, so Congress provided an important safety valve for educators and librarians.

Recall that one of the possible remedies for infringement is "statutory damages" of up to $30,000 per work infringed. Imagine you are in front of a judge who has just ruled that you are an infringer and is preparing to assess damages. Large dollar figures may be looming. The law of statutory damages, however, proceeds to give an important break for educators and librarians. In fact, the court may be required to cut the statutory damages all the way to zero. This protection applies if you are an employee or agent of a nonprofit educational institution or library, if you were acting within the scope of your employment, and you "believed and had reasonable grounds for believing" that the copies you made were "fair use." If you can meet those requirements when faced with infringement, the court must remit the statutory damages in full.[8]

> Even if statutory damages are eliminated, you are not completely off the hook. You are still an infringer subject to all other remedies, such as actual damages and injunctions. Furthermore, the exception for librarians and educators does not cover all possible uses of copyrighted materials. It only addresses reproducing the work in copies or phonorecords. No court yet has had the need to test the meaning or extent of this law.

How can you demonstrate the "reasonable grounds" about fair use? Probably the best bet is to do your homework. You might not have to become an expert, but you might have to learn a bit about fair use. You will have to apply the four factors and weigh your evaluation. You need to make a reasoned and reasonable conclusion about whether you are acting within the law. As a result, the court may still disagree with you about fair use, but the court may see your good faith and should cut your liabilities accordingly.

Who Is Liable for the Infringement?

Initially, the person who actually commits the infringement is liable. That person might be a librarian filling orders for copies, a research assistant duplicating materials for a professor, a webmaster creating a "cut-and-paste" website, or a teenager downloading music files. In general, liability begins with the person who pushes the button to make the copy or who actually commits the infringing activity.

> A company or another party can be held liable for the actions of another person on at least two theories. "Contributory infringement" can occur when someone provides the equipment or other means for creating infringements and knows, or should have known, of the infringing actions. "Vicarious liability" can occur when someone has the right to supervise the activity and stands to benefit from it; knowledge of the infringing activity is not necessary. Employers are often in similar situations, at least with respect to activities that are part of an employee's job.

In reality, in the setting of a business, library, or educational institution, liability often flows upstream to the supervisors who oversee the project and to the company or organization itself. Recall from chapter 9 the summaries of cases about fair use. The liable parties were the corporations—such as Kinko's and Texaco—and not merely the individuals. The truth is that all of the implicated individuals and organizations may share in any liability exposure.

As a practical matter, however, the supervisors and the organization are at greater risk. Not only do they more likely have "deep pockets," but a successful lawsuit at the highest level is more likely to have the greatest influence on shaping future behaviors. Suing Kinko's, for example, led to changes in photocopy practices at Kinko's shops around the country. In fact, holding the company liable helped persuade competing photocopy shops to reassess their similar practices and legal risks.

A "Safe Harbor" for Service Providers

Sometimes "contributory" or "vicarious liability" can be imposed on an online service provider (OSP). Think of America Online or another commercial service. Consider the online services provided by your own university or other organization. Can these services be held liable if they provide an e-mail or web server account and you use it to commit a copyright infringement? Is AOL liable if you download a music file and send it by e-mail to a thousand of your friends? Is the university liable if you scan your favorite book chapters and post them to your website?

The new Section 512 of the Copyright Act, creating the "safe harbor," was part of the Digital Millennium Copyright Act of 1998. That bill addressed a wide range of issues, from liability for circumvention of "technological protection systems" to a new form of legal protection for boat hulls. *Digital Millennium Copyright Act*, Public Law 105-304, *U.S. Statutes at Large* 112 (1998): 2860. Chapter 15 of this book focuses on the most important provisions of the DMCA.

So far, the answer is "maybe." The OSP can be liable, depending on the level of oversight and control and the knowledge that its officials had of the infringing activities. The reach of the law is evolving and murky.[9] Congress confronted this dilemma with new law in 1998. Congress did not exactly settle the law, but instead crafted an opportunity for OSPs to find a "safe harbor" and avoid the possible liability for copyright infringements committed by the users of the system.[10]

Generally speaking, the safe harbor usually applies only in situations where the OSP is truly passive. The statute extends to situations where the infringing materials are merely in transit through the system, cached as an automated and technical requirement of the system, or are resident on the system at the user's discretion and without the OSP's knowledge.

The new statutory protection for service providers is complicated, but it is proving to have profound consequences. To enjoy protection, the OSP must meet a lengthy list of elaborate conditions. Moreover, the "safe harbor" only protects the educational institution or other OSP itself from liability. The individuals who actually commit the infringement may still be liable. Other legal claims—trademark, privacy, libel—that arise from the same situation remain unaffected.

For educational institutions, fitting into the safe harbor may prove highly problematic. In addition to the foregoing conditions, the "safe harbor" might apply to a faculty website only if the infringing materials on the site were not "required or recommended" course materials within the last three years, and the institution has received no more than two notifications of claimed infringements committed by that faculty member. The institution must also provide all users of its system with materials that "accurately describe, and promote compliance with" copyright law.[11]

This brief summary only hints at the layers of complication in the new statute. The centerpiece of the law, however, is the procedure known as "notice and take down." For any OSP to enjoy the safe harbor, it must register an agent with the U.S. Copyright Office. The agent will then receive notices of claimed infringements. For example, suppose a professor has posted materials to her website, and the copyright owner discovers them and objects. Under this new law, the copyright owner can send a proper notice to the designated agent for that OSP.

Does your college, university, library, or other OSP have a registered agent? The full list is posted on the website of the U.S. Copyright Office at http://www.copyright.gov/onlinesp/.

In order for the online service provider to have full protection, it must then "expeditiously" remove or "take down" the infringing material from the system. The OSP may later investigate and perhaps even restore the materials if they are ultimately not a violation. But the OSP must remove them first and ask questions later. Educational institutions of all types and sizes have discovered the prevalence and power of these legal procedures. With the growth of peer-to-peer networks for posting and sharing files, copyright owners have sometimes inundated university agents with notices about the multitudes of music, movies, and other files posted by students and others on high-speed networks run by the educational institution. The administrative burden alone is leading many organizations to begin educational campaigns and sometimes to restrict student use of Internet access.

Note on Sovereign Immunity

Some copyright infringers may escape liability altogether under a sweeping constitutional doctrine. The Eleventh Amendment to the U.S. Constitution provides one more means for possibly bringing an end to all monetary risks from copyright infringement. The Eleventh Amendment provides that a state or state agency may not be sued in a federal court for dollar damages. A series of recent cases from the U.S. Supreme Court has brought renewed meaning to the provision, which is intended to protect the "sovereignty" of the states from being held accountable by a federal judiciary.[12]

Congress has attempted to eliminate or at least reduce the application of sovereign immunity. In 1990 Congress added Section 511 to the Copyright Act, explicitly declaring that states and state employees are not protected from liability. The question still remains whether Congress has the power to undercut a constitutional protection by enactment of a statute.

By an act of Congress, all copyright cases must be brought in federal court.[13] In recent years, a few federal courts accordingly have dismissed cases that were brought against states and state agencies. Of notable consequence, one court has ruled that a unit of the University of Houston (a public university) could not be sued for copyright infringement.[14]

While these developments may give some room to states and state institutions to consider the appropriateness of their activities—rather than acting out of fear of liability—these cases by no means give public institutions complete protection. They may still be liable for equitable remedies, such as injunctions. More important, if a public university acted in willful disregard of the law, it could still face criminal action.

Do the Right Thing

This chapter begins with a litany of legal risks and some disturbing dollar amounts that a copyright infringer might face. Much of this chapter, however, is about the limits of possible liability. Educators and librarians who exercise fair use in good faith may avoid statutory damages. Online service providers may find a safe harbor from infringements committed by individual users. The "sovereign immunity" provision of the U.S. Constitution may allow state agencies to avoid liability altogether. Just as important, the simple historical record is that common activities of educators and librarians have not been the target of copyright lawsuits. They are also not likely to become frequent targets in the near future.

If the chances of being sued appear slim, why should we bother paying attention to the complications of copyright at all? The answer is simple: because we live in a cooperative society, and the law is the intermediary. The law may be quirky and sometimes a little baffling, but it has an important role in shaping the terms on which we relate to one another in a civilized world. We need to give respect to the copyrights of others, if we are to gain respect for our claims of fair use.

One of the greatest virtues of American copyright law is that it allows owners and users to seek creative definitions of their rights, rather than relying solely on legal conventions. One of the best examples is Creative Commons, an initiative that encourages copyright owners to assert less than all possible legal rights, and in the process grant to the public broader rights of use. Copyright owners can select from a set of "license" terms that lay down creative rights of ownership and use. See http://creativecommons.org.

If we do not like the law, we should demand change, and we should press the law's meaning. Meanwhile, we must remind ourselves steadily that the law we challenge today may be the law that protects us in the future. Educators and librarians live in two copyright worlds at the same time. We are users of copyrighted materials, questioning the limits of fair use and seeking new exemptions for distance learning and other pursuits. Simultaneously, members of the academic community are increasingly concerned about protecting their own intellectual property. Fairness and good ethical practices demand mutual respect for the diverse interests within our own communities. In the end, we are probably best served by reasonable terms for using works as well as claiming rights.

Notes

1. The statutes governing the "remedies" or liabilities under copyright law are *U.S. Copyright Act*, 17 *U.S.C.* §§ 502–511 (2005).
2. *U.S. Copyright Act*, 17 *U.S.C.* § 504(c)(1) (2005).
3. *U.S. Copyright Act*, 17 *U.S.C.* § 505 (2005).
4. *Basic Books, Inc. v. Kinko's Graphics Corp.*, 758 F. Supp. 522 (S.D.N.Y. 1991).
5. *Basic Books, Inc. v. Kinko's Graphics Corp.*, 21 U.S.P.Q.2d 1639 (1991).
6. *U.S. Copyright Act*, 17 *U.S.C.* § 411 (2005).
7. *U.S. Copyright Act*, 17 *U.S.C.* § 506(a) (2005).
8. *U.S. Copyright Act*, 17 *U.S.C.* § 504(c)(2) (2005). As an important clarification, this statute explicitly encompasses not only educators and librarians, but also archivists.
9. See *Playboy v. Hardenburgh*, 982 F. Supp. 503 (N.D. Ohio 1997); *Religious Technology Center v. NETCOM*, 907 F. Supp. 1361 (N.D. Cal. 1995). As this book went to press, the U.S. Supreme Court handed down its ruling in *Metro-Goldwyn-Mayer Studios Inc. v. Grokster, Ltd.*, 75 U.S.P.Q.2d 1001 (U.S. 2005). The Court held that a provider of file-sharing software could be liable for infringements committed by users under some circumstances. While the Court may have added some additional clarity to the law, the issues will continue to be disputed and debated with each new development.
10. *U.S. Copyright Act*, 17 *U.S.C.* § 512 (2005).
11. For the specific provisions of the statute that apply to faculty websites, see *U.S. Copyright Act*, 17 *U.S.C.* § 512(e) (2005).
12. U.S. Constitution, amend. XI.
13. *U.S. Copyright Act*, 17 *U.S.C.* § 1338(a) (2005).
14. *Chavez v. Arte Publico Press*, 204 F.3d 601 (5th Cir. 2000).

14

Music and Copyright

KEY POINTS

- Copyright law often has a distinctive application to musical compositions and sound recordings.

- Many of the exceptions, including the first-sale doctrine and the provision for library copying, can apply to music and recordings, subject to detailed rules.

- The TEACH Act allows performances of music in distance learning, subject to important limitations.

- Performing rights societies may be helpful for licensing some educational uses of music, but not all.

Music makes the world go around, gray skies blue, blue eyes brown, and other assorted miracles happen almost daily. Music can also make even the most tranquil librarian or faculty member nearly apoplectic on occasion. Not the music itself, but more likely the "musical work" and the "sound recording" associated with it—especially as they relate to copyright law.

Like many other works, musical compositions and recordings are usually protected by copyright law. Unlike other types of works, however, compositions and recordings are often subject to a host of technical and specialized rules under American copyright statutes. These rules can become important in the search for meaningful and lawful ways to use the works in teaching, learning, and scholarship.

Why does the law—and this book—give considerable attention to music? Musical works and recordings have given rise to a legal framework underpinning an entire industry based on the protected rights of copyright owners and ostensibly attuned to meeting the market's craving for melody. For users, "musical works" are communication tools of growing importance in library collections and in support of innovative teaching and learning. Music is important to understanding society and culture. People also like music—it communicates our ideas and reveals our dreams.

The author of this chapter is Professor Dwayne K. Buttler, University Libraries, Evelyn J. Schneider Endowed Chair for Scholarly Communication, University of Louisville, Kentucky.

Musical compositions and sound recordings are often routinely eligible for copyright protection. A new composition is easily "original," and it is "fixed" when noted on paper or played into a recorder. A sound recording of the same musical composition may have originality in the rendition, style, or accompaniment. It too is "fixed" upon making the recording. For more information about these principles, see chapter 1.

Defining Music

Copyright law seeks to bring some structure amid these powerful and wondrous aspects of music. The law defines a "sound recording" as a work that results "from the fixation of a series of musical, spoken, or other sounds."[1] The law does not specifically define "musical work," but through decades of legal development, that label has generally come to refer to the composition. A "musical work" is therefore akin to a "literary work." It is the author's original creative expression, and the owner has a variety of fundamental rights to that work established under copyright law.

A "sound recording" may capture a performance of the composition, regardless of the medium or format. The recording may be on reel-to-reel tape, cassette tape, digital audiotape, MP3, or any other means for capturing the sounds. A recording is not necessarily always of music; it could also capture spoken words or other sounds—the lonesome whistle, the hoot of an owl, the roar of a jet, or the cry of a baby.

The full definition states that sound recordings are "works that result from the fixation of a series of musical, spoken, or other sounds, but not including the sounds accompanying a motion picture or other audiovisual work, regardless of the nature of the material objects, such as disks, tapes, or other phonorecords, in which they are embodied." Thus "sound recordings" exist independently of technology or format definitions and could include tin rolls, reel-to-reel, cassette, wire recorders, MP3s, and as yet unforeseen means for recording "musical, spoken, or other sounds."

—*U.S. Copyright Act, 17 U.S.C. § 101 (2005)*

We can begin to see that the composition and the recording have independent originality and fixation. The recorded "performance" of the composition becomes a sound recording and enjoys copyright protection independent of the copyright to the "musical work." A single recording therefore can contain two separate copyrighted works. Consequently, making use of the recording could affect the rights of two separate copyright owners: the composer of the song may hold a copyright in the "musical work," and the recording engineer, or more likely the recording company, may hold a copyright in the "sound recording." Understanding this interplay between musical works and sound recordings is crucial to protecting the copyrighted work and to making use of the important statutory exemptions.

Technological Evolution and Legal Frameworks

Copyright law has long had trouble keeping pace with the changing nature of music. American law did not apply to music at all until 1831.[2] That law then extended only to compositions; it did not apply to sound recordings until 1972. A century ago, the Supreme Court struggled with the copyright implications of player piano rolls, which represented a new and frightening technology. Today, the courts are addressing issues of digital file-sharing and webcasting that involve musical works and sound recordings.

Consequently, "musical works" and "sound recordings" can raise some of the most complex and frustrating quandaries in copyright law. Some distinctions in the law are unclear, some are artificial, and many are embedded in history and the relationship of new technologies to existing copyright law. In general, the law today grants the basic set of rights to copyright owners of musical works and recordings. Owners have rights of reproduction and distribution of their works. The copyright to musical works includes a general right of public performance. The owner of the sound recording has a performance right, but only in the context of a "digital audio transmission."[3]

> Until 1995, the recording enjoyed no performance right. Thus, when a recorded work of music was performed to a live audience, through broadcast or any other means, only the owner of the composition had rights—and therefore could demand payment. With the growth of online transmission, Congress granted a limited performance right to the owner of the recording. That owner can now have rights to some digital performances, but still not in other contexts. See *U.S. Copyright Act* 17 *U.S.C.* § 106(6) (2005).

As with most works, the copyright laws also carve out various exceptions to owners' rights, such as fair use. If the use fits within the requirements of an exemption, the owner cannot legally prevent the use. While the interplay of rights and exemptions is fundamental to understanding copyright protection and rights of use, the rules applied to music are sometimes distinct from general copyright standards. This chapter will summarize several major aspects of copyright law as applied to music, with emphasis on the copyright exemptions of importance to educators and librarians.

Section 108: Library Copying

Recall from chapter 12 that Section 108 of the U.S. Copyright Act permits many libraries to copy protected works for a variety of important purposes, including preservation, interlibrary loan, and private study by patrons. This exemption limits the owner's exclusive rights of reproduction and distribution. However, Section 108 does not allow libraries to copy *all* copyrighted works for *all* purposes. In particular, when libraries are making copies of "musical works" under this statute, the copies may be only for purposes of preservation and replacement.[4] Thus, under Section 108, libraries cannot make copies of musical works for patron study or for delivery through interlibrary loan.

Remember that basic point about the difference between a "musical work" and a "sound recording"? Consider these practical implications pursuant to Section 108:

- The library wants to make copies of printed sheet music, which is a form of a "musical work." The library may make copies only for preservation or replacement.
- The library wants to make copies of a sound recording of a musical performance. The library may generally copy a sound recording for any of the allowed purposes, but copying such a recording necessarily creates a copy of the underlying musical work. The library is again limited to purposes of replacement or preservation.
- The library would like to copy a sound recording of something other than music, such as a poetry reading, a political speech, or nature sounds. Because the copy does not involve a "musical work," the library may copy the recording for any of the purposes under Section 108.

As a practical matter, the library can institute preservation programs consistent with Section 108 for all recordings. But when a patron requests copies for private study, the library is limited to recordings of nonmusical works. This awkward distinction is an attempt to "balance" the rights and interests of copyright owners and copyright users. "Musical works" enjoy more protection presumably because copying them for patrons might cause market harm to the music industry. Of course, conversely, preventing these uses also might lessen the ability of libraries in some cases to fully serve the needs of some patrons for some purposes, particularly music teachers and scholars.

Section 109: The First-Sale Doctrine

Section 109 is another exemption that sometimes applies differently to musical works. Commonly known as the "first-sale" doctrine, this provision limits the copyright owner's ability to control copies—or physical embodiments—of a copyrighted work. For example, someone may own the copyright in a music CD, but the owner of a copy of that CD generally may dispose of that particular copy through any means, including giving it away, selling it, lending it, or even renting it.[5] This provision allows libraries to lend materials from their collections.

> Without the first-sale doctrine, many common activities, such as selling books, or lending them from libraries, could be unlawful "distributions" of copyrighted works. Recall from chapter 5 that distributing copies to the public is one of the rights of the copyright owner.

In the 1980s, however, the music industry became particularly alarmed by the growth of private businesses renting music CDs to the public. The obvious concern was that, unlike renting a book or many other works, a customer could rent a CD for a brief time and simply and quickly copy it. For less than a typical purchase price, someone could have a copy. Worse, the customer would then return the disk, making it available for the next customer.

Congress accordingly amended the statute to bar the first-sale doctrine as it may apply to musical works or sound recordings containing musical works, unless the lending is undertaken for "nonprofit purposes" by a "nonprofit library" or a "nonprofit educational institution."[6] "Nonprofit" is a crucial condition for meeting this exception. While it may not be defined in the statute, most academic and public libraries should easily meet this standard. As a result, most nonprofit academic libraries may continue to keep and lend their collections of sound recordings of music and other types of works.

> The lending of a "sound recording" containing a "musical work" falls outside Section 109 if the lending or rental is for the purpose of "direct or indirect commercial advantage." *U.S. Copyright Act*, 17 *U.S.C.* § 109(b)(1)(A) (2005). Notice that the limit on commercial lending only applies to certain works. The law does not bar the commercial lending of motion pictures, so your local video store may remain in business.

Section 110(2): The TEACH Act and Distance Education

Chapter 11 of this book offers considerable detail about the TEACH Act, a new statutory exception allowing uses of copyrighted works in distance education. An examination of this statute emphasizes that the law applies differently to different types of works. One important distinction in the TEACH Act surrounds the treatment of "dramatic" and "nondramatic" musical works.

Section 110(2) allows the performance of entire "nondramatic" musical works by "transmission" in the course of distance learning.[7] By contrast, the law allows performances of "dramatic" musical works only in "reasonable and limited portions." The distinction between "dramatic" and "nondramatic" music enjoys a rich and intriguing history in shaping and applying copyright law, but the law has yet to offer an explicit definition of these terms.

Understanding the meaning of "nondramatic musical works" is necessary to applying Section 110(2). We can find some insight from various sources, including this particularly pithy quotation from a leading treatise on copyright law: a "performance of a musical composition is dramatic if it aids in telling a story; otherwise, it is not."[8] Under this definition, a "musical work" might become "dramatic" if it is performed in conjunction with fixed characters, set design, staging, dance, opera, or like characteristics, but it may become "nondramatic" in the absence of such characteristics.

> The history of "dramatic" and "nondramatic" musical works is rich with nuance and rationale from copyright owners. Indeed, the Copyright Act of 1909 (which was replaced in full by the Copyright Revision Act of 1976) included a concept of "dramatico-musical" works and addressed "grand performing rights" as distinguished from "small performing rights." Moving to today's law, references in statutes and licenses to allowing performances of "nondramatic" music usually anticipate a simple, unadorned playing of instruments, singing of songs, or performances of the musical work through broadcast on radio or television. The performance often may be live, or it may be made from a preexisting recording.

While the TEACH Act expressly refers to performances of "musical works," it makes no mention of "sound recordings." This omission becomes important, however, because performing a sound recording is a common and essential means for performing a musical work. You might perform a sound recording, for example, by sliding a disk into a CD player, plopping an LP onto a turntable, or mounting an MP3 file on a website. In each situation, you are performing the underlying musical work.

The TEACH Act may not mention "sound recordings," but it does allow their performance in distance education. All works are allowed unless specifically limited or proscribed. Thus, the law creates something of a dilemma. For example, performing a "nondramatic musical work" in full is allowed, but performances of most other types of works, including sound recordings, are permissible only in "reasonable and limited portions." Therefore, if you are singing or making some other live performance of the composition, you may perform the entire work. However, if you are making the performance from a CD or other sound recording, you will be limited to "reasonable and limited portions."

Performing Rights Societies

The performance rights for "nondramatic" and "dramatic" musical works have raised other copyright complications. For historical reasons, principally the advent of radio and television broadcasting, the performance of "nondramatic" musical works has been of great importance to broadcasters and to copyright owners, who ultimately devised "licensing collectives" to "clear" permission rights and to allocate requisite royalties to copyright holders.

> Universities often secure "blanket licenses" with one or all of these licensing societies to cover many public performances of "nondramatic musical works" on campus. For more information, see the website for each organization:
>
> ASCAP: http://www.ascap.com
>
> BMI: http://www.bmi.com
>
> SESAC: http://www.sesac.com
>
> These three organizations usually license only performances of works. If you are making a new recording of an existing song, you may need to contact the Harry Fox Agency at http://www.harryfox.com.

Today, these "performing rights societies" include the American Society of Composers, Authors and Publishers (ASCAP), Broadcast Music International (BMI), and the Society of European Stage Authors and Composers (SESAC). They enjoy a nonexclusive right to "license" public performance rights in the numerous "nondramatic musical works" that each organization represents. Users may now search these song lists on the Internet. If a particular song is on a song list, the quest for permission can then be directed at the appropriate society. If the song is not on a list, then you may return to the customary search for the individual owner of the rights.

While the licensing societies can greatly streamline the process of securing permissions, the societies are generally limited to granting rights to make public performances of compositions of nondramatic music. As a result, the licenses allow only public performances and do not address reproduction or distribution rights of the musical works and sound recordings. Thus, in order to reproduce and distribute a musical work or sound recording, you may need to seek permission from the copyright owner.

> Readers will find much more information about permissions and fair use in other parts of this book. Chapter 17 is a general overview of permissions, and appendix D offers a model letter for a permission request. Chapters 7 through 10 are a detailed overview of fair use, particularly as it is important for the needs of educators and librarians.

Performing rights societies do not license performance rights in "dramatic" musical works or performance rights in sound recordings. Users generally will need to secure a license to those works directly from the copyright owner, provided that the use does not fall under an enumerated exception. Many uses within the library and academic communities may fit within one or more exemptions in the Copyright Act, including fair use.

Notes

1. *U.S. Copyright Act*, 17 *U.S.C.* § 101 (2005).
2. *Act of February 3, 1831*, ch. 16, *U.S. Statutes at Large* 4 (1831): 436.
3. *U.S. Copyright Act*, 17 *U.S.C.* § 106(6) (2005).
4. *U.S. Copyright Act*, 17 *U.S.C.* § 108(i) (2005).
5. *U.S. Copyright Act*, 17 *U.S.C.* § 106(3) (2005).
6. *U.S. Copyright Act*, 17 *U.S.C.* § 109(b)(1)(A) (2005).
7. *U.S. Copyright Act*, 17 *U.S.C.* § 110(2) (2005).
8. Melville B. Nimmer and David Nimmer, *Nimmer on Copyright*, 10 vols. (New York: Matthew Bender, 2004), § 10.10[E], pp. 10–98. See also *Robert Stigwood Group Ltd. v. Sperber*, 457 F.2d 50, 55 n.6 (2d Cir. 1972).

15

The Digital Millennium Copyright Act

KEY POINTS

- The DMCA is a major legislative enactment from 1998 that changed the U.S. Copyright Act in several important respects.

- The prohibition against circumvention of technological protection systems is perhaps the best-known and the most controversial feature of the DMCA.

- Recent court rulings may have tempered concerns that the DMCA would directly undercut fair use and other opportunities to make lawful uses of copyrighted works.

- Still, the DMCA poses tremendous challenges for educators, librarians, and others who seek ongoing access to materials that are increasingly accessible from electronic sources, and that are subject to controls and terms of license agreements.

The Digital Millennium Copyright Act, enacted October 28, 1998, is a lengthy and complex piece of legislation that modified copyright law in several important respects. It included protections for online service providers, created limited immunity for computer repair services, and launched initiatives leading to the TEACH Act for distance learning. Perhaps the most important and best-known provision of the DMCA is the statutory prohibition against the "circumvention" of technologies that control access to copyrighted works. This chapter accordingly focuses on this "anticircumvention" law as enacted in Section 1201 of the Copyright Act. Few provisions of the Copyright Act have proven so difficult to analyze and apply, leading to great uncertainty and controversy about the law. The provision may also affect access to all types of information resources, generating serious concerns among all providers and users of copyrighted materials.

When crafting the anticircumvention provisions, Congress made a broad analogy, comparing the act of breaking codes or bypassing controls as the equivalent of "breaking into a locked room in order to obtain a copy of a book."[1] Congress was in large part addressing concerns of widespread "piracy" of digital works due to "the ease with which digital works can be copied and distributed worldwide virtually instantaneously" through the Internet.[2]

Copyright owners may benefit from the new law, but educators and librarians have wondered whether its provisions will ultimately redefine access to and lawful use of copyrighted works. These debates have provoked questions about the survival of fair use and other long-standing principles of copyright law. Section 1201 may potentially alter fundamental activities such as library services, research, website development, distance education, and Internet access, thus posing enormous challenges for higher education.

> A related provision of the DMCA creates another new potential violation. Section 1202 of the Copyright Act now protects the integrity of "copyright management information," such as the title of a work, the name of its author and the copyright owner, and the terms and conditions for using the work. Removing a copyright notice or removing the names of authors from any work could be a violation if the removal conceals or allows an infringement of the copyright to that work.
>
> —*U.S. Copyright Act, 17 U.S.C. § 1202 (2005)*

The Meaning of Anticircumvention

Section 1201 creates various new potential legal liabilities. The main provision states simply: "No person shall circumvent a technological measure that effectively controls access to" a copyrighted work.[3] For example, the law would ostensibly prohibit hacking through a password interface on a database, or bypassing encrypted controls on a CD or DVD. The statute further bars the circumvention of measures that effectively control the exercise of an owner's rights in his or her copyrighted works, such as reproducing and distributing copyrighted works.[4]

In addition, Section 1201 prohibits the manufacture, distribution, or importation of a "technology, product, service, device, component, or part thereof" that is primarily designed or produced for the purpose of circumventing a technological measure.[5] In other words, not only is "circumvention" unlawful, but making and distributing software or other means for circumventing controls are also illegal.

> The sanctions for violating Sections 1201 or 1202 can be severe. Civil remedies may include injunctive relief, impoundment and modification or destruction of infringing items, statutory or actual damages, and disgorgement of profits and attorney fees. Criminal penalties may apply for willful copyright violations for the purpose of commercial advantage or private financial gain. The criminal penalties can be fines up to $500,000 or five years in prison for the first offense, and double those figures for subsequent offenses. *U.S. Copyright Act, 17 U.S.C. §§ 1203, 1204 (2005)*. The statutes include some limitations on penalties for educational institutions, libraries, archives, and public broadcasters.

Litigation and Enforcement of the DMCA

In the several years since enactment of the DMCA, the anticircumvention law has developed in perhaps surprising and unexpected directions.

Cases in the News

Section 1201 has given rise to several court cases that suggest potentially disturbing applications of the law. The following two examples were covered prominently in the news and in professional literature, although the courts ultimately did not make extensive rulings on the substantive meaning of the anticircumvention law.[6]

The Prosecution of Elcomsoft and Dmitry Sklyarov

One of the first cases involving an alleged violation of the DMCA was a criminal case brought against Dmitry Sklyarov, a Russian immigrant, and Elcomsoft, an affiliated company. Sklyarov and Elcomsoft were charged with distributing software that could enable users to bypass the encryption technology used to protect Adobe electronic books. They faced a variety of criminal charges, including conspiracy to traffic in technological systems that were designed and marketed primarily to circumvent measures protecting a right of a copyright owner (pursuant to Section 1201(b)(1)(C)). Sklyarov was released from federal custody after entering into an agreement with the United States attorney. In late 2002, a jury acquitted Elcomsoft of criminal copyright charges.

> In the *Elcomsoft* case, the act of circumvention was specifically intended to allow the application of software that could enable a user to transfer an electronic book to another computer, to make a print or backup copy of it, or to hear or "audibly read" the e-book. In an interesting development, the regulations from the Librarian of Congress, summarized later in this chapter, created an exemption from the anticircumvention law for the purposes of making an e-book audible. Thus, while the DMCA appeared to have a stringent effect in its early years, later developments have tempered its consequences.

Professor Felten and the Music Challenge

Professor Edward Felten of Princeton University responded to a public challenge from the Secure Digital Music Initiative (SDMI), which had invited experts to analyze the security of an SDMI "digital watermark" copy-prevention system. Felten and his research team successfully found a means to circumvent the SDMI technological controls. When Felten sought to publish his findings, he faced legal threats from SDMI. The claim was that under the DMCA, his research paper was a circumvention device because it purported to describe how the SDMI technology works. The Electronic Freedom Foundation supported Professor Felten and initiated legal action in federal court, asking the court to declare that publishing a research paper was not a violation of the DMCA. When the music industry dropped its threats against Felten, the court dismissed his case.

The Felten and Sklyarov cases did not result in elaborate rulings about the substantive merits of the DMCA, but other situations have led to litigation and interpretive rulings from various courts. While these cases seem to have little if any relevance to librarians and educators, they do offer important insights into the meaning of the law and its possible application in future situations.

Cases in the Courts

Litigation surrounding the meaning and application of Section 1201 has expanded significantly in recent years. The following cases demonstrate something about the law's evolution and offer some insights about its meaning for educators and librarians.

Universal City Studios, Inc. v. Reimerdes, 111 F. Supp. 2d 294 (S.D.N.Y. 2000), aff'd sub nom. *Universal City Studios, Inc. v. Corley*, 273 F.3d 429 (2d Cir. 2001)

A group of movie studios sought an injunction under the DMCA, charging that the defendant was sharing software that could enable users to view DVD movies on different operating systems. Each DVD included a "content scrambling system" (CSS) that permitted the film to be played, but not copied, only on certain players that incorporated the plaintiffs' licensed decryption technology. CSS, therefore, was a means for controlling access to the copyrighted content on the disk. The defendant's website included a link to other sites where users could find and download "DeCSS." That program allowed users to circumvent the CSS protective system and to view the film on other DVD players. Once circumventing CSS, users could also copy the motion picture, and not merely view it.

> Another recent case revealed the potential reach of Section 1201, although the court did not find a violation under the particular circumstances. Lexmark is a well-known producer of computer printers, and its cartridges include a computer chip with embedded code. The code ensures that only "authorized" replacement cartridges can be used with Lexmark printers. The defendant made and sold "gray-market" cartridges with a chip that could interact with the copyrighted code in Lexmark printers. The court found no violation of the DMCA, because buyers of Lexmark printers could, if they desired, open the copyrighted code. The replacement cartridges, therefore, did not circumvent any effective controls on obtaining or reading the code. Nevertheless, this case suggests that had Lexmark more effectively "locked" the code inside its printers, it might well have been able to use the DMCA to eliminate competition for its printer cartridges.
>
> —*Lexmark International, Inc. v. Static Control Components, Inc.*, 387 F.3d 522 (6th Cir. 2004)

The court found the defendant had violated the anticircumvention law by making DeCSS available on its websites. The court may have been influenced by the fact that the DVDs could be copied once they were accessed using DeCSS. Nevertheless, the actual violation stems from the use of systems for access alone. In other words, even if users would only play the motion picture from the DVD, which was perfectly legal, a violation of Section 1201 might still occur. This case demonstrates that the DMCA can prevent even lawful activities, if the user must circumvent the access system to reach the needed content.

Chamberlain Group, Inc. v. Skylink Technologies, Inc., 381 F.3d 1178 (Fed. Cir. 2004)

While the *Reimerdes* case appeared to establish a far-reaching right for copyright owners—perhaps allowing them to assert copyright infringement against users who bypass access controls under nearly any circumstance—the *Chamberlain* case tempered that view in various important respects. The court made clear that the access right was confined to situations in which access was "unauthorized." The court placed the burden on the copyright owner to prove that the user accessed the copyrighted work for a purpose that was not authorized either by the owner or by law. In other words, if the ultimate purpose of circumventing the technological measure was to enjoy what would otherwise be a lawful access or use of the copyrighted work, no violation of the DMCA may have occurred.

The case's factual context reveals much about the new law—and it demonstrates that garage doors have something in common with library research. Skylink manufactured a universal remote control that could operate garage openers made by various companies, including openers made by Chamberlain. Chamberlain charged that Skylink's device violated the DMCA, asserting that for Skylink's remote to function, it had to circumvent copyrighted computer codes embedded in Chamberlain's equipment. The court disagreed, finding that owners of Chamberlain's openers fully expect to have access to the codes—through the use of a remote control—in order for any remote to function properly. Moreover, nothing in the garage door opener itself, or in the customer agreement, barred the necessary access. Therefore, when Skylink accessed the codes, it was not engaged in any unlawful use of the copyrighted work.

> The U.S. Copyright Act provides this definition: "to 'circumvent a technological measure' means to descramble a scrambled work, to decrypt an encrypted work, or otherwise to avoid, bypass, remove, deactivate, or impair a technological measure, without the authority of the copyright owner."
> —*U.S. Copyright Act*, 17 *U.S.C.* § 1201(a)(3)(A) (2005)

This case offers an important interpretation of Section 1201 that may have profound and positive consequences for librarians, researchers, and others concerned about the effects of the DMCA. The court in *Chamberlain* turned to the statutory definition of "circumvent" and noted that it included an explicit reference to *unauthorized* access. The court accordingly ruled that a "circumvention" under the DMCA can occur only when the ultimate access is one that creates a violation, or is at least "reasonably related" to a violation of the owner's reproduction rights or other rights under the Copyright Act. The court also underscored that the DMCA should not be used to erode fair use or other sanctioned activities; thus, bypassing the technological controls for such lawful ends may not be a violation of Section 1201.

The *Chamberlain* case goes far to take some of the threat out of Section 1201. The court's fresh reconsideration of the law is built on solid reasoning and good public policy. The court's interpretations also fit nicely with the normal functioning of software in such things as garage door openers. As we use these devices, we deploy the software with the simple click of a button. Normal operations pose little realistic opportunity to copy the software or to make other improper use of it. The *Chamberlain* case further emphasizes that the situation in *Reimerdes* was quite different. While users of the DVDs in *Reimerdes* might only have watched the movie—a lawful

> The *Chamberlain* case breathed life into this provision of the anticircumvention law: "Nothing in this section shall affect rights, remedies, limitations, or defenses to copyright infringement, including fair use, under this title." *U.S. Copyright Act*, 17 *U.S.C.* § 1201(c)(1) (2005). The court concluded that this language means that circumventing protection systems to engage in fair use must have been anticipated by Congress.

activity—the circumvention of the controls also allowed users to copy the movie. Accordingly, bypassing codes for unlawful ends, such as unauthorized reproduction, could remain a violation of the DMCA under the reasoning of both *Reimerdes* and *Chamberlain*.

Exceptions for Libraries and Education

Amidst uncertainties surrounding the effect of the "anticircumvention" law, Congress sought to alleviate some of these concerns by creating several complex exceptions to the law. A few of them are specifically for the benefit of higher education. Some exceptions were enacted as part of the original DMCA; other exceptions are created periodically by regulations from the Librarian of Congress.

> The DMCA includes a few additional exceptions for purposes such as accessing information for law enforcement. *U.S. Copyright Act*, 17 *U.S.C.* § 1201(e) (2005). Of interest to some educators is a provision allowing the reverse engineering of programs to create interoperability with other programs. *U.S. Copyright Act*, 17 *U.S.C.* § 1201(f) (2005). Another provision allows researchers to decrypt security codes for the purpose of identifying and analyzing "flaws and vulnerabilities." *U.S. Copyright Act*, 17 *U.S.C.* § 1201(g) (2005). Again, the statutes are rigorous and narrow. Use of these provisions could be perilous without detailed legal advice.

Statutory Exceptions

Upon enactment of the DMCA, Congress carved out for libraries the authority to circumvent technological protections if the purpose is to access and review the protected work in good faith for purposes of determining whether or not to purchase it.[7] Like most exceptions to anticircumvention, this one is qualified by multiple detailed conditions. The exemption is narrowly and meticulously constructed, and a library is subject to serious legal penalties if it utilizes the exemption but is later determined to have misapplied the law.[8] One has to seriously question whether the benefits of attempting to use this exemption will outweigh the accompanying risks of possible liability.

Perhaps the biggest drawbacks of the exception are its immediate practical implications. The exception may be used only to review copyrighted works with an eye toward possible purchase; many reputable vendors will allow such a review or sampling without hesitation. Ultimately, anyone using the exception is proposing to "hack" through the password or other protective system. Few reputable libraries will want to keep hackers on hand and turn them loose on commercial databases.

Regulatory Exceptions

The Librarian of Congress has the authority to issue periodic exceptions to the anticircumvention law. During the initial two years after enactment, and every three years thereafter, the Librarian of Congress, upon recommendation of the Register of Copyrights, is required to conduct proceedings to examine and review the effect of the DMCA on the availability and use of copyrighted works, notably for education and libraries. Specifically, the Librarian of Congress is empowered to identify particular classes of works and particular users who would be "adversely affected" if the restrictions of the DMCA prevented their making "noninfringing uses" of those works.[9]

> Under the terms of Section 1201(a)(1)(C), the Librarian of Congress is directed to develop new regulatory exceptions every three years. Hence, the next regulations are expected in late 2006, then in late 2009, and so on. Each round is a new opportunity for educators and librarians to gather data and to urge the Librarian to make a new exception that meets real and important needs.

In late 2000, the Librarian of Congress announced a rulemaking that listed two classes of works as exempt from the anticircumvention law:

- Compilations consisting of lists of Internet locations that are blocked by commercially marketed filtering systems
- Literary works that are protected by access control mechanisms, but those mechanisms fail to function properly, preventing the intended access[10]

In late 2003, the Librarian of Congress completed a second round of rulemaking and announced a continuation and modification of the existing exemptions. The Librarian also identified two other classes of exempted works:

- Computer programs protected by dongles that prevent access due to malfunction or damage and which are obsolete
- Computer programs and video games distributed in formats that have become obsolete and which require the original media or hardware as a condition of access[11]

Outlook for Libraries and Education

In practice, the DMCA still facilitates the imposition of controls on uses of copyrighted works. The law also reinforces the use of contracts to set standards for allowable uses of the materials. For example, libraries have long purchased journals, made them widely available to the public, and allowed multiple readers to benefit from the works and to make "fair use" of them. New technologies now allow the same journals (and many other works) to be acquired through electronic databases, which ordinarily employ passcodes or other limits on access.

Under those circumstances, copyright owners have the ability to define who may access the databases and to restrict and impose conditions or fees for each use. Shortcutting those controls could violate the DMCA, with the practical consequence of allowing legally enforceable controls on the utility of library resources. Owners can deny access to users who do not assent to all stipulated restrictions. Owners may insist on restrictions that attempt to constrain public access, fair use, and other virtues of copyright law.

The *Chamberlain* case infuses hope into the future meaning of the DMCA by allowing some "circumvention" when the end purpose is fair use or other lawful activity. Although the *Chamberlain* decision is an important and good development in the law, it does not do away with many problems of the DMCA for librarians and educators. However, if *Chamberlain* means that a user can circumvent access controls, if ultimately the copyrighted work is used lawfully, these possibilities might be permitted under the reasoning of *Chamberlain*:

- A user may be able to use or adjust the controls of a DVD player in order to watch films from disks that have "region code" restrictions. Private viewing of copyrighted films is not a copyright violation.

- A user might be able to remove anti-copying code on disks storing software or other copyrighted works, if the ultimate purpose is to load the materials onto a computer or even copy it in full, and if the copy is deemed to be within fair use or another exception.

- A library may be able to bypass or disable similar controls, if the purpose is to make a preservation copy consistent with Section 108 of the Copyright Act.

> "Region codes" are often embedded with DVD movies and computer game disks to restrict use of the work to a designated region of the world. A buyer of a DVD in Europe, for example, would be blocked from playing that disk in a machine purchased in North America. In *Sony Computer Entertainment America Inc. v. Gamemasters*, 87 F. Supp. 2d 976 (N.D. Cal. 1999), the defendant created a "Game Enhancer" which allowed users of a Sony PlayStation to play games on machines which were not from the designated region. The court held that enabling users to bypass territory codes was a form of circumventing access controls. Because the simple act of using a disk from another country is not a violation of U.S. law, one has to wonder if a court would find a DMCA violation for that reason alone in the aftermath of *Chamberlain*.

- An educator may be able to circumvent controls in order to copy and deliver materials in distance education, consistent with the terms and limits of the TEACH Act in Section 110(2) of the Copyright Act.

Perhaps these uses would be allowed. We are a long way from knowing if the law will develop in these directions, but the *Chamberlain* case is an important harbinger of the DMCA's possibilities. The *Chamberlain* decision suggests that such lawful activities may ultimately not be subverted by copyright owners who impose overburdening restrictions on their works.

> Because access to content will increasingly be subject to the terms of license agreements, the librarian or other professional responsible for negotiating and approving licenses may become the most important member of the organization. That person will be in a position to determine whether users will have access to content at all and the terms on which the materials may be used.

Nevertheless, the most serious dilemmas of the DMCA continue, even if the *Chamberlain* reasoning is applied broadly. In order to make any lawful uses of works that are kept behind technological controls, the earnest educator, librarian, or other user still has to make the decision—and have the know-how—to circumvent whatever controls exist. Perhaps more ominously, that honest user has to be ready to decide that the circumvention is within the law. For if he or she is wrong, the DMCA can impose steep civil penalties and criminal sanctions—including time in prison. Even in the best of circumstances, the DMCA can be a serious and continuing cloud on proper access to and use of copyrighted works.

Notes

1. *Digital Millennium Copyright Act*, 105th Cong., 2d sess. (1998). H. Doc. 551: 17–18.
2. *Digital Millennium Copyright Act*, 105th Cong., 2d sess. (1998). S. Doc. 190: 8.
3. *U.S. Copyright Act*, 17 *U.S.C.* § 1201(a)(1)(A) (2004).
4. *U.S. Copyright Act*, 17 *U.S.C.* § 1201(b) (2004).
5. *U.S. Copyright Act*, 17 *U.S.C.* §§ 1201(a)(2) and (b) (2004).
6. In the *Elcomsoft* case, a court did rule on the constitutionality of the DMCA provisions. *U.S. v. Elcom, Ltd.*, 203 F. Supp. 2d 1111 (N.D. Cal. 2002).
7. *U.S. Copyright Act*, 17 *U.S.C.* § 1201(d) (2005).
8. *U.S. Copyright Act*, 17 *U.S.C.* § 1201(d)(3) (2005).
9. *U.S. Copyright Act*, 17 *U.S.C.* §§ 1201(a)(1)(C)–(D) (2005).
10. *Code of Federal Regulations*, title 37, vol. 1, sec. 201.40 (2005).
11. *Code of Federal Regulations*, title 37, vol. 1, sec. 201.40.

16

Copyright and Unpublished Materials

KEY POINTS

- Unpublished works can include manuscripts, computer programs, and a wide variety of materials of importance to education and librarianship.

- Congress eliminated the perpetual "common-law" copyright protection that previously applied, and unpublished works are today subject to federal copyright protection.

- In general, the duration of protection for unpublished works is the same as for other works, meaning that the copyrights in unpublished works from long ago may expire.

- Fair use can apply to unpublished works, but it usually applies narrowly as compared to other types of works.

- Some other provisions of the Copyright Act, notably Section 108, include distinctive rules applicable to unpublished works.

Unpublished works can range from historical manuscripts to modern research findings and computer programming. In many instances, copyright law applies a distinctive set of rules to such works, often resulting in tighter controls on their use. Sometimes the reasons for the law are built on sound policies of confidentiality or privacy. The author of private correspondence and journals may have extraordinary need for greater control over writings that may disclose confidences. Memoranda in business files may contain trade secrets. Many computer programs may be selectively utilized or licensed and were never meant for wide distribution or publication. Other unpublished works are simply not quite ready for full disclosure. They may be drafts of articles or raw film footage not yet refined into the final published version. Special protection for these works is sometimes easy to justify.

The history of copyright law includes important precedents for the distinctive treatment of unpublished materials. Today the rights of copyright owners include rights of "reproduction" and more. But early cases often spoke of a "right of publication" or a "right of first publication."[1] Controlling when a work would be allowed to reach the market and have full disclosure was generally safeguarded for the author's benefit.

The logic of these developments is fairly simple. Concerns about confidentiality often lead to greater protection and hence usually a more constrained allowance of fair use or other public rights of use. Whether that explanation is valid or not, it has shaped copyright law in several respects, generally resulting in greater protection for unpublished works. This chapter will focus on a few aspects of current copyright law that are specifically applicable to unpublished works, and that are of particular importance to librarians, educators, and researchers.

Duration of Protection

Before 1978, unpublished works were not protected under federal copyright law at all. The application of federal "statutory" copyright protection began to apply only upon publication of the book, music, or other work. If the work was published with a proper copyright notice, then statutory protection would apply for a period of years. If the publication lacked the requisite notice, the work immediately entered the public domain.

> Chapter 3 of this book details the rules and terms of copyright duration. Before 1978, "statutory" copyright protection began with a term of twenty-eight years. It could then be renewed. Under current law, such early works could have protection for as long as ninety-five years.

Up to the time of publication, however, the work enjoyed something known as "common-law" copyright protection. This protection was not part of federal law, but the rights were instead generally recognized and enforced under state law. Common-law protection applied automatically, and one of its most significant traits was that it lasted indefinitely. More bluntly, it would last in perpetuity—forever—as long as the work remained unpublished. The author might have been dead for centuries, but the copyright lived on. Common-law copyright posed serious challenges for anyone working with unpublished materials, such as the biographer needing to quote from letters and diaries or wanting to reprint a family snapshot. The legal protection was strong, and even letters from centuries ago still had valid copyrights.

With the full revision of the U.S. Copyright Act, effective January 1, 1978, Congress brought an end to much of the problem. Congress abolished common-law copyright and brought all eligible works—published or not—under federal copyright protection.[2] Moreover, Congress eliminated the perpetual protection and applied the basic terms of protection to new and old works that are unpublished.[3] For the first time in American history, the copyrights to unpublished works could now expire. For the first time, researchers could anticipate that unpublished materials—including diaries, letters, survey responses, e-mail correspondence, manuscripts, photographs, art, and software—would eventually enter the public domain and become available for unrestricted use.

Still, Congress did not make the law easy. To understand the duration rules for unpublished works, we still need to separate works created before and after the beginning of 1978. For unpublished works created since that date, we can apply the general rules of duration:

- For works created by individual authors, the copyright lasts for the life of the author, plus 70 years.[4]

- In the case of works made for hire, the duration for unpublished works is generally 120 years from the date of creation. If the work is eventually published, the copyright duration will be the lesser of either 120 years from creation or 95 years from publication.[5]

> The duration rules that apply to works made for hire also apply to anonymous and pseudonymous works. Many unpublished works routinely lack a clear identification of authors. The works might be scribbles, missives, scrapbooks, or other cryptic products.

What about unpublished works from before 1978? Even works from the earliest years of American history? Congress laid down the general proposition that the general, current duration rules apply to those materials as well, although Congress postponed application of those rules until January 1, 2003.[6] As of that date, a wealth of unpublished materials entered the public domain for the first time. For example:

- Your archive may include letters and diaries written by Thomas Jefferson (died in 1826), Frederick Douglass (died in 1895), or Louisa May Alcott (died in 1888). Because the writers died more than seventy years ago, the copyrights in their unpublished works have lapsed. You may reprint the materials in full and upload them into a digital library without copyright restriction.
- You are writing the history of Mega Corporation, and you have files of memos written by company founders in the nineteenth century. If the writings are "for hire" and are more than 120 years old, they are no longer under copyright protection.
- You are planning to publish a book about the Civil War and want to include a set of photographs from the 1860s, but you cannot identify the photographer. If the work is indeed "anonymous," the copyright expired after 120 years.

Again, however, Congress did not make the law quite so easy. One more important twist in this law remains. Congress postponed the new law—as applied to unpublished materials—until 2003 in order to give rightful copyright owners an opportunity to find and benefit from copyright protection. Copyright owners by that time were typically family members or others who received the copyright through transfer or inheritance. In the years leading up to 2003, Congress offered an important inducement to owners: find and publish the works before 2003, make them available to the public, and the law will reward you with additional years of rights.[7]

Consider this actual example. Samuel Clemens, also known as Mark Twain, died in 1910. A previously unpublished chapter of his novel *Huckleberry Finn* was discovered in the 1990s. A new edition of *Huckleberry Finn* was published in 2001 with the "missing" chapter integrated into the full book.[8] The original portions, published in 1884, had entered the public domain decades earlier and remain there. Copyright protection for the "unpublished" chapter, however, might have expired in 1980, seventy years after Twain's demise. But that rule did not take effect until 2003, and because the chapter was published before the end of 2002, the law gave it an additional forty-five years of copyright protection, to the end of 2047.

Researchers accordingly must be watchful of two common possibilities. First, you might find a manuscript or other "unpublished" work from the past, but before you can conclude that it is in the public domain, you need to research whether in fact it might have been published in the meantime. Second, you may find a published work, such as a novel from the distant past, but some pieces of it may well have been added more recently and will enjoy protection under copyright law.

Fair Use of Unpublished Works

A series of court rulings through the last two decades have established a relatively narrow application of fair use to unpublished works. The issue has been of enormous importance to the software industry and other parties, whose works are often kept "unpublished" and are worth enormous amounts of money. Yet most judicial decisions have been about the use of letters, diaries, and other resources central to the writing of history and biography. When courts ruled in the late 1980s that biographers may not be within fair use when making customary quotations from letters written by J. D. Salinger and L. Ron Hubbard, researchers expressed alarm.[9]

Congress responded in 1992 by adding this sentence to the fair-use statute: "The fact that a work is unpublished shall not itself bar a finding of fair use if such finding is made upon consideration of all the above factors."[10] Congress was striving to dissuade the courts from making a complete bar on fair use for unpublished works, and the effort appeared to work. Subsequent cases have allowed authors to make limited quotations from the journal of Richard Wright and the manuscripts of Marjorie Rawlins.[11]

While fair use has found new meaning in the context of unpublished works, that meaning remains somewhat circumscribed. In all of the cases, courts have tipped the "nature" factor firmly against a finding of fair use, reasoning that the "unpublished nature" of the materials means that they merit greater protection. Courts have built these principles on a presumption that letters, diaries, and other manuscripts may include private information, and stronger protection allows the copyright owner to choose whether, when, and how to make the works publicly available.

The recent cases were provoked by a decision from the U.S. Supreme Court in the *Harper & Row* case, which involved the use of quotations from the manuscript of Pres. Gerald Ford's memoirs. The Court ruled that the quotations were not within the limits of fair use, in large part because the memoirs were not yet published. The Court articulated a "right of first publication" and held that fair use applies narrowly when it could effectively erode the author's ability to choose when to publish, or even whether to publish the materials at all.[12]

> Despite a narrow construction of fair use applied to private letters and similar materials, some interesting examples continue to brush the limits of fair use. For example, when a set of letters written by J. D. Salinger to a former romantic acquaintance was sold at auction, sizable excerpts appeared in the *New York Times*. The newspaper also quoted heavily from letters by Thomas Pynchon, another reclusive author, when they were added to the research collections of the Pierpont Morgan Library. For more information about these and other examples, see Kenneth D. Crews, "Fair Use of Unpublished Works: Burdens of Proof and the Integrity of Copyright," *Arizona Law Journal* 31 (Spring 1999): 1–93.

> In 1985 the U.S. Supreme Court ruled in *Harper & Row Publishers, Inc. v. Nation Enterprises*, 471 U.S. 539 (1985), that fair use applied narrowly to an unpublished book manuscript, in order to preserve the "right of first publication." Recall from chapter 5 that copyright owners have certain rights set forth in Section 106 of the Copyright Act. The "right of first publication" is not among them. Where did the Supreme Court find this right? It had long been a feature of the common law of copyright as applied to unpublished materials. The U.S. Copyright Act preempts the common law. Nevertheless, the Court breathed life into what could have been an obsolete doctrine.

The following cases illustrate the recent evolution of the fair-use law for unpublished works.

Salinger v. Random House, Inc., 811 F.2d 90 (2d Cir. 1987)

Random House was preparing to publish a biography of the famous and reclusive author J. D. Salinger, and the book was to include quotations from private correspondence available to researchers in various manuscript collections. Salinger wrote the letters, and recipients had donated the materials to libraries at Harvard, Princeton, and other universities. The lower court had ruled that the limited quotations and paraphrases were within fair use, but the court of appeals disagreed, circumscribing sharply the application of fair use to unpublished materials. The court seemed particularly moved by the apparent personal or confidential nature of the letters, as well as their literary qualities. These considerations affected all four of the factors.

Purpose: The court agreed that the purpose of the use was "criticism," or "scholarship," or "research." Any of these purposes would favor a finding of fair use, even in the context of a book that would likely be published and sold for commercial gain. On the other hand, the court gave no special leniency for biographers who might customarily depend on quoting from private letters to tell an important story.

Nature: Here the court succinctly and firmly leaned against fair use for unpublished materials.

Amount: The court also held the biographer to a highly restrictive standard, finding that many of the quotations used more of Salinger's expression than was "necessary to disseminate the facts." The court appeared to be deeply influenced by the literary qualities of Salinger's letters, finding infringements even when the quotations were limited to mere phrases and even paraphrasing of the originals.

Effect: The court relied on testimony about the monetary value of the letters, or the possibility that Salinger or his successors might choose to publish them in the future, to conclude that quotations in a published biography could harm those speculative markets.

Sundeman v. Seajay Society, Inc., 142 F.3d 194 (4th Cir. 1998)

The *Salinger* case suggested that the unpublished nature of the work could greatly influence the analysis of all four factors. Researchers began to see in *Salinger* nearly a total elimination of fair use. The *Sundeman* case, however, reveals that much had changed in the law by the late 1990s. Today, this case is an important reminder that reasonable, limited, scholarly uses of unpublished materials may well be within fair use.

The *Sundeman* decision involved the use of significant quotations from a manuscript by the author Marjorie Rawlins. A researcher at a nonprofit foundation selected quotations from the unpublished manuscript and included those quotations in an analytical presentation delivered to a scholarly society. Turning to the four factors, the court ruled that the researcher was acting within fair use.

Purpose: Her use was scholarly, transformative, and provided criticism and comment on the original manuscript. All of these purposes worked in favor of fair use. The court especially noted that moving the excerpts from the original novel to the context of scholarly criticism was a "transformative" use.

Nature: The court relied on a long series of cases to resolve that the "unpublished" nature of the work "militates against" fair use. On the other hand, the court pointed to the new language in the fair-use statute, and emphasized that the use of unpublished works may still be within the law.

Amount: The amount of the work used was consistent with the purpose of scholarly criticism and commentary, and the use did not take "the heart of the work," as has been important in other cases. The court was also not concerned that the amount copied was between 4 and 6 percent.

Effect: The court found no evidence that the presentation displaced any market for publishing the original work, and a presentation at a scholarly conference may in fact have increased demand for the full work.

The Current Trend

These cases reflect the trend away from an apparent "per se" bar on fair use for unpublished works. When Congress added the language about unpublished works, it was striving to eliminate any notion of a complete bar on fair use. In other rulings, courts have found fair use when a biographer quoted from the personal journals of Richard Wright, and when an author of a critical study printed excerpts from rap lyrics written by Eminem before he found fame.[13] Fair use does apply to unpublished works today, and it often will allow brief or moderate quotations, as are customary for research in history, biography, and many other disciplines.

> By detailing Section 108 as applicable to the preservation of unpublished works, Congress was laying out a distinctive scope of user rights. In many other statutory exceptions, however, the law does not specify whether the works used may be published or unpublished. For example, Sections 110(1) and 110(2) address displays and performances of works in the classroom and in distance education. By not stipulating that the work must be published, the law apparently applies equally to the use of unpublished works.

Library Preservation and Other Statutory Exceptions

Recall from chapter 6 that the Copyright Act includes numerous statutory exceptions to the rights of owners. A few of them have some implications for the use of unpublished works. Most notable is Section 108, which allows many libraries to make limited copies of works for specific purposes (see chapter 12 of this book). One of those purposes is for preservation programs, and here the statute outlines a distinctive application to preservation copies of unpublished materials. The rules are not necessarily more rigorous than the rules applicable to published works. They are just different.

When librarians make preservation copies of published works, they must search the market for a replacement before making a new copy. The rule is logical: as long as the work is still published, libraries should be ready to buy replacements, rather than make their own. By contrast, if the work is unpublished, no such market exists. The unpublished work, however, may be personal or confidential. Consequently, the library may make the copy, but usually only to retain it in the library for research and study—and not for wide dissemination.

Promoting Progress

This chapter is an overview of certain aspects of copyright law applicable to unpublished materials. These examples provide important demonstrations of the underlying principles and functions of copyright. Copyright law serves two pragmatic purposes: to protect creative works, and to facilitate beneficial uses of those works by the public. These purposes are often in conflict with one another. Through the last two centuries, Congress has steadily reevaluated the tension and has struck new legal articulations of a balance between the law's purposes.

When applied to unpublished materials, the law sometimes establishes a distinct balance, reflecting the particular interests of copyright owners and the singular importance of unpublished materials for research, education, and other pursuits. When Congress eliminates perpetual copyright protection for manuscripts, or applies a limited fair use to personal diaries, it is striving to achieve the broadest goal of copyright law—to promote the progress of science and learning. In that spirit, Congress has moved away from rigid and absolute bars on the uses of unpublished works. Instead, the law has migrated toward a bit of flexibility and ultimately a fresh rethinking and adjustment of owners' and users' rights.

Notes

1. *Harper & Row Publishers, Inc. v. Nation Enterprises*, 471 U.S. 539 (1985); *Estate of Martin Luther King, Jr., Inc. v. CBS, Inc.*, 194 F.3d 1211 (11th Cir. 1999).
2. *U.S. Copyright Act*, 17 *U.S.C.* § 301(a) (2005).
3. *U.S. Copyright Act*, 17 *U.S.C.* §§ 302–304 (2005).
4. In the case of works created by joint authors, the copyright lasts through the life of the last of the authors to die, plus seventy more years. *U.S. Copyright Act*, 17 *U.S.C.* § 302 (2005).
5. *U.S. Copyright Act*, 17 *U.S.C.* § 302(c) (2005).
6. *U.S. Copyright Act*, 17 *U.S.C.* § 303 (2005).
7. *U.S. Copyright Act*, 17 *U.S.C.* § 303.
8. Mark Twain, *Adventures of Huckleberry Finn*, ed. Victor Fisher and Lin Salamo, with Walter Blair (Berkeley: University of California Press, 2001).
9. *Salinger v. Random House, Inc.*, 811 F.2d 90 (2d Cir. 1987); *New Era Publications International v. Henry Holt and Co.*, 695 F. Supp. 1493 (S.D.N.Y. 1988), *aff'd*, 873 F.2d 576 (2d Cir. 1989).
10. *Fair Use and Unpublished Works Act*, Public Law 102-492, *U.S. Statutes at Large* 106 (1992): 3145, codified at 17 *U.S.C.* § 107 (2005).
11. *Wright v. Warner Books, Inc.*, 953 F.2d 731 (2d Cir. 1991); *Sundeman v. Seajay Society, Inc.*, 142 F.3d 194 (4th Cir. 1998).
12. *Harper & Row Publishers, Inc. v. Nation Enterprises*, 471 U.S. 539 (1985).
13. *Wright v. Warner Books, Inc.*, 953 F.2d 731; *Shady Records, Inc. v. Source Enterprises, Inc.*, 2005 WL 14920 (S.D.N.Y. 2005).

17

Permission from Copyright Owners

KEY POINTS

- No permission is needed if your work is in the public domain, or if your use is within fair use or another exception.

- Permission for some works may be available through a collective licensing agency.

- Contacting a copyright owner and drafting a permission letter can involve a careful strategy.

- You still have options after reaching a "dead end" in your quest.

Copyright law grants broad rights to copyright owners and then "carves out" exceptions to them, such as fair use. While these exceptions are extremely valuable for maintaining a balance between owners and the public, not all planned uses of copyrighted works will fit within one of these statutory possibilities. In that event, users may seek a license—or permission—from the copyright owner allowing use of the work.

This chapter describes a step-by-step process for obtaining permission to use copyrighted works. It provides insights for streamlining the process and strategies for dealing with problems that commonly occur when making permission requests.

Specify the Work and the Planned Use

The first step in obtaining permission to use a copyrighted work is to identify precisely the work in question and your planned uses of it. When selecting a work, stay flexible and consider substitutions that may meet your needs. Copyright owners are free to deny permission requests or to require a licensing fee that may be outside your budget. Also, finding and eliciting a response from copyright owners can sometimes prove difficult or impossible. Having multiple works to draw upon will improve your chances of success.

You do not need to seek or secure permission if your use is within fair use or another exception. Study the exceptions summarized in chapters 6, 7, 8, 11, and 12 of this book. The fundamental point of the exceptions is that the public may use the works without permission and without incurring liability. Seeking permission may at times be good courtesy. From another perspective, however, seeking permission for activity within fair use is not only unnecessary but may be counterproductive.

In addition, stay flexible about your precise uses of the work. For example, you might have a great plan to digitize photos and make them available on a website. The owner may object to broad access and require limitations on the photos' use. Similarly, the owner may oppose the making of digital copies, but will allow you to make print versions. Explore alternatives with the owner as necessary.

Determine Whether Permission Is Required

Permission may not be necessary for many reasons, but a common reason is that the work is not protected by copyright at all. A work may be in the public domain for a myriad of reasons. If it is, you may use it freely and without copyright restriction. Early research concerning the copyright status of a work could save you considerable time and money.

Several other chapters of this book detail the possibilities for determining whether a work is in the public domain. Some materials are never protected, such as facts, unoriginal compilations, and works produced by the U.S. government

Check to see if permission for your use is already authorized by the copyright owner. Often libraries purchase videos with a license to use them in educational performances. Sometimes colleges and universities acquire full-text databases under contracts that permit a variety of educational uses. Many publications have statements of permission printed on the introductory pages. A little checking could spare you the burden of tracking down the copyright owner.

Identify and Contact the Copyright Owner

You can determine the identity of the copyright owner by several methods. You would do best to start with the work itself. It may include a copyright notice indicating the original claimant of the copyright. While the copyright notice is a good place to start your investigation, remember that copyright ownership may have been transferred, leaving some notices out-of-date and inaccurate.

The records at the U.S. Copyright Office may be helpful in determining the copyright owner. Copyright owners seeking the fullest protection of their works will often register claims with the Copyright Office. Registration, however, is not a prerequisite for protection, so the public records are hardly complete. Also, the Copyright Office may list one party as the owner, but the ownership may since have been transferred, with no record of the disposition. Again, documents at the Copyright Office can be incomplete and outdated.

The U.S. Copyright Office's records may be searched to help determine the copyright status of a work. Newer records may be searched for online for free. For a fee, the Copyright Office will conduct searches for you. The Copyright Office's website, at http://www.copyright.gov, includes detailed information about searches.

All too often, the quest for the copyright owner is akin to a detective venture. The original author may have transferred the copyright to a publisher. That publisher may have sold its assets, including copyrights, to another company. In other cases, the original author may have retained the copyright, but died and left the estate, including copyrights, to an assortment of family members. Sometimes you just have to persevere and engage in a series of telephone calls to authors, editors, and family members.

Some copyright owners have eased the search. They may act through various collective licensing agencies that serve as "agents" for multiple copyright owners. Publishers of books and journals often use the Copyright Clearance Center. Some musical works are licensed through agencies such as ASCAP or BMI. If an organization represents the copyright owner, it may offer a license directly to you. In other instances, the organization may put you in direct contact with the owner. Licenses available through these agencies are often available simply by submitting the request and paying the licensing fee online.

> The Copyright Clearance Center can help expedite some licensing processes. Through its website, you may request permission to make certain uses of thousands of works, including books, magazines, journal articles, newsletters, and dissertations. Permission fees are paid directly to the CCC and are then forwarded to the appropriate copyright owners. The Copyright Clearance Center's website is at http://www .copyright.com. The use of ASCAP, BMI, and other music licensing agencies is examined in chapter 14.

Large publishers and television networks sometimes have their own permission departments to handle licensing requests. These departments may be contacted via an e-mail address available on the company's website. Many of these departments offer standard permission request forms that you may complete and submit through the mail or online.

Draft a Permission Request

Ultimately, you often have to contact copyright owners directly, either by e-mail or the postal service. An advance telephone call will often assure that you are writing to the proper owner. That call may also signal whether or not the permission will likely be forthcoming.

As you prepare the permission letter, consider choosing one of the following two strategies for drafting your request.

> Whenever possible, secure grants of permission in writing. Oral permission may be allowed under the law, but a written and signed document will be important in case of any misunderstandings between you and the copyright owner.

Specific request. Many copyright owners insist on a detailed request, and the permission will be limited accordingly. For example, if you request permission to make print copies of a work during the next semester of your course, the permission will not cover digital scans, posting the item to the course website, or using it in subsequent semesters. Copyright owners often require elaborate information in order to determine fees or whether to grant permission at all. Omitting pertinent information in your request may delay permission.

General request. Sometimes a little flexibility in your permission can be helpful. Open-ended and broad language may offer more flexibility to meet changing needs. For example, if you can anticipate using the work in repeated semesters for various projects, you might ask for broad rights to "use the work in connection with my teaching." Accordingly, you might not specify such matters as:

- A termination date for the permission
- A maximum number of students using the work
- The medium by which you will share the work (i.e., electronic or print)
- The specific nature of the use (i.e., distance education or face-to-face teaching)

One obvious downside of this strategy is that the copyright owner may ask for more information, leading to delays.

Whatever method or means you use to secure permission, you need to be ready to address these important points:

How much: The price that copyright owners will charge for use of their works is difficult if not impossible to estimate. Some licensing fees will be exorbitant and cost-prohibitive, yet other copyright owners may be happy to grant permission at little or no cost. You usually just have to ask. Owners may base fees on the type of use or the number of people who may have access to their works. You should be ready to provide the details, if you can.

What: Cite the precise work, and the exact portion of the work you wish to use. The fee to use a portion of a work may be less than the fee for the use of the entire work. For text works, include the exact pages, sections, or chapters you plan to use. For sound recordings and audiovisual works, include a detailed description of the portion and length you wish to use.

When: The copyright owner may want to know when and for how long you plan on using the work. Some owners may be wary of granting permission for extended periods of time or for dates far in the future.

Why: The purpose of your use may be critical to determining the licensing fee or whether permission is granted at all. Owners tend to be more supportive of nonprofit classroom uses, but if you are planning to include the material in a publication or on an open website, you will likely need to offer those details.

How: The proliferation of alternatives for using copyrighted works has caused many owners to insist on detailed plans. You might have to specify whether you are making classroom handouts or sending the materials to a commercial printer for duplication. Some owners will want to know if you will deliver the works electronically, and if your course-management system is password-protected.

> The terms of your licensing agreement are only limited by your imagination and the willingness of the parties to reach agreement. Contemplate all your possible uses—present and future—and request permission accordingly.

The "Dead End" of Permission Quests

Too often, your effort to secure permission reaches a "dead end." This disappointing conclusion may take many forms. You may never find the copyright owner; the copyright owner may never respond to your request; the licensing fee may be cost-prohibitive; or the copyright owner may bluntly deny permission. Dead ends are common occurrences and can be extremely frustrating. Consider the following strategies for addressing such circumstances.

> Chapter 13 includes an overview of the risks and liabilities of copyright infringement. That chapter also describes some important protections for educators and librarians who are acting in good faith. One practical point to emphasize here is that liabilities may be limited if the work is not registered with the Copyright Office. Some users may also have additional protections if they conduct a good-faith application of fair use.

Return to fair use. The fair-use analysis that you conducted before seeking permission should have been based in part on the potential effect that your use would have on the market for the work. Reaching a dead end may suggest that your use will cause little or no market harm. Armed with this new information, a new fair-use analysis may now have a different result.

Replace the planned work with alternative materials. Substitute works may satisfy your needs. Look for works in the public domain or works for which permission is more likely to be forthcoming. Also, consider creating your own work and avoid having to ask for permission altogether.

Alter your planned use of the work. Some copyright owners will deny certain types of use or deny permission to copy large portions of a work. Revise your plans to accommodate the owner's requirements. For example, request to use a smaller portion of the work, or deliver the work to students via a password-protected system rather than a public website.

Conduct a risk-benefit analysis. Sometimes you face the difficult need to assess whether using the work is worth the risk of stirring legal claims. Your assessment should carefully weigh a number of factors, including the importance of making the exact intended use; how openly "exposed" your use of the work will be; and the thoroughness of your investigation and the diligence of your attempts to request permission. Undertaking such an analysis should be done with great caution. The effort can pose serious legal and ethical quandaries. Educators and librarians may want to consider notifying supervisors or asking legal counsel to assist in such an analysis. Unfortunately, copyright owners are often elusive, leaving users to face such difficult decisions.

A Selected Provisions from the U.S. Copyright Act

The Congress of the United States has the power to make copyright law. The earliest federal copyright legislation dates to 1790, and Congress has revised the Copyright Act at various times since then. In 1976 Congress made the most recent complete revision of the federal copyright laws, enacting statutes that replaced the existing code and that took effect on January 1, 1978. Current law is therefore often referred to as the "Copyright Act of 1976." As readers of this book can surmise, Congress has amended the Copyright Act of 1976 many times since then. In fact, between 1976 and 2005, Congress enacted approximately fifty bills that have changed the current Copyright Act. Some of the changes have been minor, while others have been profound and complicated.

This appendix reprints selected provisions from the current U.S. Copyright Act. The statutes are included principally because of their relevance to the issues covered by this book. Consequently, readers will find here the statutes related to the rights of owners and the statutes on fair use and other public rights of use. The author has added the language that is in brackets.

The full text of the U.S. Copyright Act is available from many sources. The website of the U.S. Copyright Office includes a link to the full act as well as links to individual bills (such as the Digital Millennium Copyright Act) and to helpful explanations of copyright law (such as the "circulars" and other materials). Visit that website at http://www.copyright.gov.

Section 101. Definitions

Section 102. Subject Matter of Copyright: In General

Section 103. Subject Matter of Copyright: Compilations and Derivative Works

Section 105. Subject Matter of Copyright: United States Government Works

Section 106. Exclusive Rights in Copyrighted Works

Section 107. Limitations on Exclusive Rights: Fair Use

Section 108. Limitations on Exclusive Rights: Reproduction by Libraries and Archives

Section 109. Limitations on Exclusive Rights: Effect of Transfer of Particular Copy or Phonorecord

Section 110. Limitations on Exclusive Rights: Exemption of Certain Performances and Displays

Section 114. Scope of Exclusive Rights in Sound Recordings

Section 504. Remedies for Infringement: Damages and Profits

Section 1201. Circumvention of Copyright Protection Systems

Section 101. Definitions

[The importance of the definitions should not be overlooked. For example, Section 105 states that a work of the U.S. government is not protected by copyright. To determine the reach of that provision, one must look to the definition of a "work of the United States Government" in Section 101. Nothing in Section 105 will tell the reader to look to the definitions, so anyone working with the Copyright Act must be familiar with the words and concepts that are defined in the law. To make the matter more interesting, some provisions of the Copyright Act include their own definitions of selected terms, apart from the definitions in Section 101. For example, this appendix includes Section 110, which includes some definitions. The following definitions are only selected excerpts from Section 101 as may be important to the readers of this book.]

"Audiovisual works" are works that consist of a series of related images which are intrinsically intended to be shown by the use of machines or devices such as projectors, viewers, or electronic equipment, together with accompanying sounds, if any, regardless of the nature of the material objects, such as films or tapes, in which the works are embodied.

A "collective work" is a work, such as a periodical issue, anthology, or encyclopedia, in which a number of contributions, constituting separate and independent works in themselves, are assembled into a collective whole.

A "compilation" is a work formed by the collection and assembling of preexisting materials or of data that are selected, coordinated, or arranged in such a way that the resulting work as a whole constitutes an original work of authorship. The term "compilation" includes collective works.

A "computer program" is a set of statements or instructions to be used directly or indirectly in a computer in order to bring about a certain result.

"Copies" are material objects, other than phonorecords, in which a work is fixed by any method now known or later developed, and from which the work can be perceived, reproduced, or otherwise communicated, either directly or with the aid of a machine or device. The term "copies" includes the material object, other than a phonorecord, in which the work is first fixed.

A work is "created" when it is fixed in a copy or phonorecord for the first time; where a work is prepared over a period of time, the portion of it that has been fixed at any particular time constitutes the work as of that time, and where the work has been prepared in different versions, each version constitutes a separate work.

A "derivative work" is a work based upon one or more preexisting works, such as a translation, musical arrangement, dramatization, fictionalization, motion picture version, sound recording, art reproduction, abridgment, condensation, or any other form in which a work may be recast, transformed, or adapted. A work consisting of editorial revisions, annotations, elaborations, or other modifications, which, as a whole, represent an original work of authorship, is a "derivative work."

A "digital transmission" is a transmission in whole or in part in a digital or other non-analog format.

To "display" a work means to show a copy of it, either directly or by means of a film, slide, television image, or any other device or process or, in the case of a motion picture or other audiovisual work, to show individual images nonsequentially.

A "joint work" is a work prepared by two or more authors with the intention that their contributions be merged into inseparable or interdependent parts of a unitary whole.

"Literary works" are works, other than audiovisual works, expressed in words, numbers, or other verbal or numerical symbols or indicia, regardless of the nature of the material objects, such as books, periodicals, manuscripts, phonorecords, film, tapes, disks, or cards, in which they are embodied.

To "perform" a work means to recite, render, play, dance, or act it, either directly or by means of any device or process or, in the case of a motion picture or other audiovisual work, to show its images in any sequence or to make the sounds accompanying it audible.

A "performing rights society" is an association, corporation, or other entity that licenses the public performance of nondramatic musical works on behalf of copyright owners of such works, such as the American Society of Composers, Authors and Publishers (ASCAP), Broadcast Music, Inc. (BMI), and SESAC, Inc.

"Phonorecords" are material objects in which sounds, other than those accompanying a motion picture or other audiovisual work, are fixed by any method now known or later developed, and from which the sounds can be perceived, reproduced, or otherwise communicated, either directly or with the aid of a machine or device. The term "phonorecords" includes the material object in which the sounds are first fixed.

"Pictorial, graphic, and sculptural works" include two-dimensional and three-dimensional works of fine, graphic, and applied art, photographs, prints and art reproductions, maps, globes, charts, diagrams, models, and technical drawings, including architectural plans. Such works shall include works of artistic craftsmanship insofar as their form but not their mechanical or utilitarian aspects are concerned; the design of a useful article, as defined in this section, shall be considered a pictorial, graphic, or sculptural work only if, and only to the extent that, such design incorporates pictorial, graphic, or sculptural features that can be identified separately from, and are capable of existing independently of, the utilitarian aspects of the article.

"Publication" is the distribution of copies or phonorecords of a work to the public by sale or other transfer of ownership, or by rental, lease, or lending. The offering to distribute copies or phonorecords to a group of persons for purposes of further distribution, public performance, or public display, constitutes publication. A public performance or display of a work does not of itself constitute publication.

To perform or display a work "publicly" means—

(1) to perform or display it at a place open to the public or at any place where a substantial number of persons outside of a normal circle of a family and its social acquaintances is gathered; or

(2) to transmit or otherwise communicate a performance or display of the work to a place specified by clause (1) or to the public, by means of any device or process, whether the members of the public capable of receiving the performance or display receive it in the same place or in separate places and at the same time or at different times.

"Sound recordings" are works that result from the fixation of a series of musical, spoken, or other sounds, but not including the sounds accompanying a motion picture or other audiovisual work, regardless of the nature of the material objects, such as disks, tapes, or other phonorecords, in which they are embodied.

A "transfer of copyright ownership" is an assignment, mortgage, exclusive license, or any other conveyance, alienation, or hypothecation of a copyright or of any of the exclusive rights comprised in a copyright, whether or not it is limited in time or place of effect, but not including a nonexclusive license.

To "transmit" a performance or display is to communicate it by any device or process whereby images or sounds are received beyond the place from which they are sent.

A "work of visual art" is—

(1) a painting, drawing, print or sculpture, existing in a single copy, in a limited edition of 200 copies or fewer that are signed and consecutively numbered by the author, or, in the case of a sculpture, in multiple cast, carved, or fabricated sculptures of 200 or fewer that are consecutively numbered by the author and bear the signature or other identifying mark of the author; or

(2) a still photographic image produced for exhibition purposes only, existing in a single copy that is signed by the author, or in a limited edition of 200 copies or fewer that are signed and consecutively numbered by the author.

A work of visual art does not include—

(A)(i) any poster, map, globe, chart, technical drawing, diagram, model, applied art, motion picture or other audiovisual work, book, magazine, newspaper, periodical, data base, electronic information service, electronic publication, or similar publication;

(ii) any merchandising item or advertising, promotional, descriptive, covering, or packaging material or container;

(iii) any portion or part of any item described in clause (i) or (ii);

(B) any work made for hire; or

(C) any work not subject to copyright protection under this title.

A "work of the United States Government" is a work prepared by an officer or employee of the United States Government as part of that person's official duties.

A "work made for hire" is—

(1) a work prepared by an employee within the scope of his or her employment; or

(2) a work specially ordered or commissioned for use as a contribution to a collective work, as a part of a motion picture or other audiovisual work, as a translation, as a supplementary work, as a compilation, as an instructional text, as a test, as answer material for a test, or as an atlas, if the parties expressly agree in a written instrument signed by them that the work shall be considered a work made for hire. For the purpose of the foregoing sentence, a "supplementary work" is a work prepared for publication as a secondary adjunct to a work by another author for the purpose of introducing, concluding, illustrating, explaining, revising, commenting upon, or assisting

in the use of the other work, such as forewords, afterwords, pictorial illustrations, maps, charts, tables, editorial notes, musical arrangements, answer material for tests, bibliographies, appendixes, and indexes, and an "instructional text" is a literary, pictorial, or graphic work prepared for publication and with the purpose of use in systematic instructional activities.

[*The definition of a "work made for hire" includes some additional language emphasizing that paragraph (2) of the definition shall not be interpreted with reference to a congressional bill from 1999 that added "sound recordings" to the list, but was quickly repealed in 2000. The law develops in some peculiar ways.*]

Section 102. Subject Matter of Copyright: In General

(a) Copyright protection subsists, in accordance with this title, in original works of authorship fixed in any tangible medium of expression, now known or later developed, from which they can be perceived, reproduced, or otherwise communicated, either directly or with the aid of a machine or device. Works of authorship include the following categories:

(1) literary works;

(2) musical works, including any accompanying words;

(3) dramatic works, including any accompanying music;

(4) pantomimes and choreographic works;

(5) pictorial, graphic, and sculptural works;

(6) motion pictures and other audiovisual works;

(7) sound recordings; and

(8) architectural works.

(b) In no case does copyright protection for an original work of authorship extend to any idea, procedure, process, system, method of operation, concept, principle, or discovery, regardless of the form in which it is described, explained, illustrated, or embodied in such work.

Section 103. Subject Matter of Copyright: Compilations and Derivative Works

(a) The subject matter of copyright as specified by section 102 includes compilations and derivative works, but protection for a work employing preex-

isting material in which copyright subsists does not extend to any part of the work in which such material has been used unlawfully.

(b) The copyright in a compilation or derivative work extends only to the material contributed by the author of such work, as distinguished from the preexisting material employed in the work, and does not imply any exclusive right in the preexisting material. The copyright in such work is independent of, and does not affect or enlarge the scope, duration, ownership, or subsistence of, any copyright protection in the preexisting material.

Section 105. Subject Matter of Copyright: United States Government Works

Copyright protection under this title is not available for any work of the United States Government, but the United States Government is not precluded from receiving and holding copyrights transferred to it by assignment, bequest, or otherwise.

Section 106. Exclusive Rights in Copyrighted Works

Subject to sections 107 through 122, the owner of copyright under this title has the exclusive rights to do and to authorize any of the following:

(1) to reproduce the copyrighted work in copies or phonorecords;

(2) to prepare derivative works based upon the copyrighted work;

(3) to distribute copies or phonorecords of the copyrighted work to the public by sale or other transfer of ownership, or by rental, lease, or lending;

(4) in the case of literary, musical, dramatic, and choreographic works, pantomimes, and motion pictures and other audiovisual works, to perform the copyrighted work publicly;

(5) in the case of literary, musical, dramatic, and choreographic works, pantomimes, and pictorial, graphic, or sculptural works, including the individual images of a motion picture or other audiovisual work, to display the copyrighted work publicly; and

(6) in the case of sound recordings, to perform the copyrighted work publicly by means of a digital audio transmission.

Section 107. Limitations on Exclusive Rights: Fair Use

Notwithstanding the provisions of sections 106 and 106A, the fair use of a copyrighted work, including such use by reproduction in copies or phonorecords or by any other means specified by that section, for purposes such as criticism, comment, news reporting, teaching (including multiple copies for classroom use), scholarship, or research, is not an infringement of copyright. In determining whether the use made of a work in any particular case is a fair use the factors to be considered shall include—

(1) the purpose and character of the use, including whether such use is of a commercial nature or is for nonprofit educational purposes;

(2) the nature of the copyrighted work;

(3) the amount and substantiality of the portion used in relation to the copyrighted work as a whole; and

(4) the effect of the use upon the potential market for or value of the copyrighted work.

The fact that a work is unpublished shall not itself bar a finding of fair use if such finding is made upon consideration of all the above factors.

Section 108. Limitations on Exclusive Rights: Reproduction by Libraries and Archives

(a) Except as otherwise provided in this title and notwithstanding the provisions of section 106, it is not an infringement of copyright for a library or archives, or any of its employees acting within the scope of their employment, to reproduce no more than one copy or phonorecord of a work, except as provided in subsections (b) and (c), or to distribute such copy or phonorecord, under the conditions specified by this section, if—

(1) the reproduction or distribution is made without any purpose of direct or indirect commercial advantage;

(2) the collections of the library or archives are (i) open to the public, or (ii) available not only to researchers affiliated with the library or archives or with the institution of which it is a part, but also to other persons doing research in a specialized field; and

(3) the reproduction or distribution of the work includes a notice of copyright that appears on the copy or phonorecord that is reproduced under the provisions of this section, or includes a legend stating that the work may be protected by copyright if no such notice can be found on the copy or phonorecord that is reproduced under the provisions of this section.

(b) The rights of reproduction and distribution under this section apply to three copies or phonorecords of an unpublished work duplicated solely for purposes of preservation and security or for deposit for research use in another library or archives of the type described by clause (2) of subsection (a), if—

(1) the copy or phonorecord reproduced is currently in the collections of the library or archives; and

(2) any such copy or phonorecord that is reproduced in digital format is not otherwise distributed in that format and is not made available to the public in that format outside the premises of the library or archives.

(c) The right of reproduction under this section applies to three copies or phonorecords of a published work duplicated solely for the purpose of replacement of a copy or phonorecord that is damaged, deteriorating, lost, or stolen, or if the existing format in which the work is stored has become obsolete, if—

(1) the library or archives has, after a reasonable effort, determined that an unused replacement cannot be obtained at a fair price; and

(2) any such copy or phonorecord that is reproduced in digital format is not made available to the public in that format outside the premises of the library or archives in lawful possession of such copy.

For purposes of this subsection, a format shall be considered obsolete if the machine or device necessary to render perceptible a work stored in that format is no longer manufactured or is no longer reasonably available in the commercial marketplace.

(d) The rights of reproduction and distribution under this section apply to a copy, made from the collection of a library or archives where the user makes his or her request or from that of another library or archives, of no more than one article or other contribution to a copyrighted collection or periodical issue, or to a copy or phonorecord of a small part of any other copyrighted work, if—

(1) the copy or phonorecord becomes the property of the user, and the library or archives has had no notice that the copy or phonorecord would be used for any purpose other than private study, scholarship, or research; and

(2) the library or archives displays prominently, at the place where orders are accepted, and includes on its order form, a warning of copyright in accordance with requirements that the Register of Copyrights shall prescribe by regulation.

(e) The rights of reproduction and distribution under this section apply to the entire work, or to a substantial part of it, made from the collection of a library or archives where the user makes his or her request or from that of another library or archives, if the library or archives has first determined, on the basis of a reasonable investigation, that a copy or phonorecord of the copyrighted work cannot be obtained at a fair price, if—

(1) the copy or phonorecord becomes the property of the user, and the library or archives has had no notice that the copy or phonorecord would be used for any purpose other than private study, scholarship, or research; and

(2) the library or archives displays prominently, at the place where orders are accepted, and includes on its order form, a warning of copyright in accordance with requirements that the Register of Copyrights shall prescribe by regulation.

(f) Nothing in this section—

(1) shall be construed to impose liability for copyright infringement upon a library or archives or its employees for the unsupervised use of reproducing equipment located on its premises: *Provided*, That such equipment displays a notice that the making of a copy may be subject to the copyright law;

(2) excuses a person who uses such reproducing equipment or who requests a copy or phonorecord under subsection (d) from liability for copyright infringement for any such act, or for any later use of such copy or phonorecord, if it exceeds fair use as provided by section 107;

(3) shall be construed to limit the reproduction and distribution by lending of a limited number of copies and excerpts by a library or archives of an audiovisual news program, subject to clauses (1), (2), and (3) of subsection (a); or

(4) in any way affects the right of fair use as provided by section 107, or any contractual obligations assumed at any time by the library or archives when it obtained a copy or phonorecord of a work in its collections.

(g) The rights of reproduction and distribution under this section extend to the isolated and unrelated reproduction or distribution of a single copy or phonorecord of the same material on separate occasions, but do not extend to cases where the library or archives, or its employee—

(1) is aware or has substantial reason to believe that it is engaging in the related or concerted reproduction or distribution of multiple copies or phonorecords of the same material, whether made on one occasion or over a period of time, and whether intended for aggregate use by one or more individuals or for separate use by the individual members of a group; or

(2) engages in the systematic reproduction or distribution of single or multiple copies or phonorecords of material described in subsection (d): *Provided*, That nothing in this clause prevents a library or archives from participating in interlibrary arrangements that do not have, as their purpose or effect, that the library or archives receiving such copies or phonorecords for distribution does so in such aggregate quantities as to substitute for a subscription to or purchase of such work.

(h)(1) For purposes of this section, during the last 20 years of any term of copyright of a published work, a library or archives, including a nonprofit educational institution that functions as such, may reproduce, distribute, display, or perform in facsimile or digital form a copy or phonorecord of such work, or portions thereof, for purposes of preservation, scholarship, or research, if such library or archives has first determined, on the basis of a reasonable investigation, that none of the conditions set forth in subparagraphs (A), (B), and (C) of paragraph (2) apply.

(2) No reproduction, distribution, display, or performance is authorized under this subsection if—

(A) the work is subject to normal commercial exploitation;

(B) a copy or phonorecord of the work can be obtained at a reasonable price; or

(C) the copyright owner or its agent provides notice pursuant to regulations promulgated by the Register of Copyrights that either of the conditions set forth in subparagraphs (A) and (B) applies.

(3) The exemption provided in this subsection does not apply to any subsequent uses by users other than such library or archives.

(i) The rights of reproduction and distribution under this section do not apply to a musical work, a pictorial, graphic or sculptural work, or a motion picture or other audiovisual work other than an audiovisual work dealing with news, except that no such limitation shall apply with respect to rights granted by subsections (b), (c), and (h), or with respect to pictorial or graphic works published as illustrations, diagrams, or similar adjuncts to works of which copies are reproduced or distributed in accordance with subsections (d) and (e).

Section 109. Limitations on Exclusive Rights: Effect of Transfer of Particular Copy or Phonorecord

(a) Notwithstanding the provisions of section 106(3), the owner of a particular copy or phonorecord lawfully made under this title, or any person authorized by such owner, is entitled, without the authority of the copyright owner, to sell or otherwise dispose of the possession of that copy or phonorecord. Notwithstanding the preceding sentence, copies or phonorecords of works subject to restored copyright under section 104A that are manufactured before the date of restoration of copyright or, with respect to reliance parties, before publication or service of notice under section 104A(e), may be sold or otherwise disposed of without the authorization of the owner of the restored copyright for purposes of direct or indirect commercial advantage only during the 12-month period beginning on—

(1) the date of the publication in the *Federal Register* of the notice of intent filed with the Copyright Office under section 104A(d)(2)(A), or

(2) the date of the receipt of actual notice served under section 104A(d)(2)(B), whichever occurs first.

(b)(1)(A) Notwithstanding the provisions of subsection (a), unless authorized by the owners of copyright in the sound recording or the owner of copyright in a computer program (including any tape, disk, or other medium embodying such program), and in the case of a sound recording in the musical works embodied therein, neither the owner of a particular phonorecord nor any person in possession of a particular copy of a computer program (including any tape, disk, or other medium embodying such program), may, for the purposes of direct or indirect commercial advantage, dispose of, or authorize the disposal of, the possession of that phonorecord or computer program (including any tape, disk, or other medium embodying such program) by rental, lease, or lending, or by any other act or practice in the nature of rental, lease, or lending. Nothing in the preceding sentence shall apply to the rental, lease, or lending of a phonorecord for nonprofit purposes by a nonprofit library or nonprofit educational institution. The transfer of possession of a lawfully made copy of a computer program by a nonprofit educational institution to another nonprofit educational institution or to faculty, staff, and students does not constitute rental, lease, or lending for direct or indirect commercial purposes under this subsection.

(B) This subsection does not apply to—

(i) a computer program which is embodied in a machine or product and which cannot be copied during the ordinary operation or use of the machine or product; or

(ii) a computer program embodied in or used in conjunction with a limited purpose computer that is designed for playing video games and may be designed for other purposes.

(C) Nothing in this subsection affects any provision of chapter 9 of this title.

(2)(A) Nothing in this subsection shall apply to the lending of a computer program for nonprofit purposes by a nonprofit library, if each copy of a computer program which is lent by such library has affixed to the packaging containing the program a warning of copyright in accordance with requirements that the Register of Copyrights shall prescribe by regulation.

(B) Not later than three years after the date of the enactment of the Computer Software Rental Amendments Act of 1990, and at such times thereafter as the Register of Copyrights considers appropriate, the Register of Copyrights, after consultation with representatives of copyright owners and librarians, shall submit to the Congress a report stating whether this paragraph has achieved its intended purpose of maintaining the integrity of the copyright system while providing nonprofit libraries the capability to fulfill their function. Such report shall advise the Congress as to any information or recommendations that the Register of Copyrights considers necessary to carry out the purposes of this subsection.

(3) Nothing in this subsection shall affect any provision of the antitrust laws. For purposes of the preceding sentence, "antitrust laws" has the meaning given that term in the first section of the Clayton Act and includes section 5 of the Federal

Trade Commission Act to the extent that section relates to unfair methods of competition.

(4) Any person who distributes a phonorecord or a copy of a computer program (including any tape, disk, or other medium embodying such program) in violation of paragraph (1) is an infringer of copyright under section 501 of this title and is subject to the remedies set forth in sections 502, 503, 504, 505, and 509. Such violation shall not be a criminal offense under section 506 or cause such person to be subject to the criminal penalties set forth in section 2319 of title 18.

(c) Notwithstanding the provisions of section 106(5), the owner of a particular copy lawfully made under this title, or any person authorized by such owner, is entitled, without the authority of the copyright owner, to display that copy publicly, either directly or by the projection of no more than one image at a time, to viewers present at the place where the copy is located.

(d) The privileges prescribed by subsections (a) and (c) do not, unless authorized by the copyright owner, extend to any person who has acquired possession of the copy or phonorecord from the copyright owner, by rental, lease, loan, or otherwise, without acquiring ownership of it.

(e) Notwithstanding the provisions of sections 106(4) and 106(5), in the case of an electronic audiovisual game intended for use in coin-operated equipment, the owner of a particular copy of such a game lawfully made under this title, is entitled, without the authority of the copyright owner of the game, to publicly perform or display that game in coin-operated equipment, except that this subsection shall not apply to any work of authorship embodied in the audiovisual game if the copyright owner of the electronic audiovisual game is not also the copyright owner of the work of authorship.

Section 110. Limitations on Exclusive Rights: Exemption of Certain Performances and Displays

Notwithstanding the provisions of section 106, the following are not infringements of copyright:

(1) performance or display of a work by instructors or pupils in the course of face-to-face teaching activities of a nonprofit educational institution, in a classroom or similar place devoted to instruction, unless, in the case of a motion picture or other audiovisual work, the performance, or the display of individual images, is given by means of a copy that was not lawfully made under this title, and that the person responsible for the performance knew or had reason to believe was not lawfully made;

(2) except with respect to a work produced or marketed primarily for performance or display as part of mediated instructional activities transmitted via digital networks, or a performance or display that is given by means of a copy or phonorecord that is not lawfully made and acquired under this title, and the transmitting government body or accredited nonprofit educational institution knew or had reason to believe was not lawfully made and acquired, the performance of a nondramatic literary or musical work or reasonable and limited portions of any other work, or display of a work in an amount comparable to that which is typically displayed in the course of a live classroom session, by or in the course of a transmission, if—

(A) the performance or display is made by, at the direction of, or under the actual supervision of an instructor as an integral part of a class session offered as a regular part of the systematic mediated instructional activities of a governmental body or an accredited nonprofit educational institution;

(B) the performance or display is directly related and of material assistance to the teaching content of the transmission;

(C) the transmission is made solely for, and, to the extent technologically feasible, the reception of such transmission is limited to—

(i) students officially enrolled in the course for which the transmission is made; or

(ii) officers or employees of governmental bodies as a part of their official duties or employment; and

(D) the transmitting body or institution—

(i) institutes policies regarding copyright, provides informational materials to faculty, students, and relevant staff members that accurately describe, and promote compliance with, the laws of the United States relating to copyright, and provides notice to students that materials used in connection with the course may be subject to copyright protection; and

(ii) in the case of digital transmissions—

(I) applies technological measures that reasonably prevent—

(aa) retention of the work in accessible form by recipients of the transmission from the transmitting body or institution for longer than the class session; and

(bb) unauthorized further dissemination of the work in accessible form by such recipients to others; and

(II) does not engage in conduct that could reasonably be expected to interfere with technological measures used by copyright owners to prevent such retention or unauthorized further dissemination;

[*Most of the remainder of Section 110 creates exceptions, generally allowing performances and displays of works, but only under specific conditions and for specific types of users. Among the users who have the benefit of these provisions are religious organizations, restaurants, horticultural organizations, and blind and handicapped persons. Section 110 continues with the following language, applicable to Section 110(2) about distance education.*]

In paragraph (2), the term "mediated instructional activities" with respect to the performance or display of a work by digital transmission under this section refers to activities that use such work as an integral part of the class experience, controlled by or under the actual supervision of the instructor and analogous to the type of performance or display that would take place in a live classroom setting. The term does not refer to activities that use, in 1 or more class sessions of a single course, such works as textbooks, course packs, or other material in any media, copies or phonorecords of which are typically purchased or acquired by the students in higher education for their independent use and retention or are typically purchased or acquired for elementary and secondary students for their possession and independent use.

For purposes of paragraph (2), accreditation—

(A) with respect to an institution providing post-secondary education, shall be as determined by a regional or national accrediting agency recognized by the Council on Higher Education Accreditation or the United States Department of Education; and

(B) with respect to an institution providing elementary or secondary education, shall be as recognized by the applicable state certification or licensing procedures.

For purposes of paragraph (2), no governmental body or accredited nonprofit educational institution shall be liable for infringement by reason of the transient or temporary storage of material carried out through the automatic technical process of a digital transmission of the performance or display of that material as authorized under paragraph (2). No such material stored on the system or network controlled or operated by the transmitting body or institution under this paragraph shall be maintained on such system or network in a manner ordinarily accessible to anyone other than anticipated recipients. No such copy shall be maintained on the system or network in a manner ordinarily accessible to such anticipated recipients for a longer period than is reasonably necessary to facilitate the transmissions for which it was made.

Section 114. Scope of Exclusive Rights in Sound Recordings

(a) The exclusive rights of the owner of copyright in a sound recording are limited to the rights specified by clauses (1), (2), (3) and (6) of section 106, and do not include any right of performance under section 106(4).

(b) The exclusive right of the owner of copyright in a sound recording under clause (1) of section 106 is limited to the right to duplicate the sound recording in the form of phonorecords or copies that directly or indirectly recapture the actual sounds fixed in the recording. The exclusive right of the owner of copyright in a sound recording under clause (2) of section 106 is limited to the right to prepare a derivative work in which the actual sounds fixed in the sound recording are rearranged, remixed, or otherwise altered in sequence or quality. The exclusive rights of the owner of copyright in a sound recording under clauses (1) and (2) of section 106 do not extend to the making or duplication of another sound recording that consists entirely of an independent fixation of other sounds, even though such sounds imitate or simulate those in the copyrighted sound recording. The exclusive rights of the owner of copyright in a sound recording under clauses (1), (2), and (3) of section 106 do not apply to sound recordings included in educational television and radio programs (as defined in section 397 of title 47) distributed or transmitted by or through public broadcasting entities (as defined by section 118(g)): *Provided,* That copies or phonorecords of said programs are not commercially distributed by or through public broadcasting entities to the general public.

(c) This section does not limit or impair the exclusive right to perform publicly, by means of a phonorecord, any of the works specified by section 106(4).

[Section 114(d) is an unduly complicated provision, stretching for a dozen or more pages, that sets forth the conditions under which the copyright in a sound recording may have the benefit of a performance right pursuant to Section 106(6).]

Section 504. Remedies for Infringement: Damages and Profits

(a) IN GENERAL.—Except as otherwise provided by this title, an infringer of copyright is liable for either—

(1) the copyright owner's actual damages and any additional profits of the infringer, as provided by subsection (b); or

(2) statutory damages, as provided by subsection (c).

(b) ACTUAL DAMAGES AND PROFITS.—The copyright owner is entitled to recover the actual damages suffered by him or her as a result of the infringement, and any profits of the infringer that are attributable to the infringement and are not taken into account in computing the actual damages. In establishing the infringer's profits, the copyright owner is required to present proof only of the infringer's gross revenue, and the infringer is required to prove his or her deductible expenses and the elements of profit attributable to factors other than the copyrighted work.

(c) STATUTORY DAMAGES.—

(1) Except as provided by clause (2) of this subsection, the copyright owner may elect, at any time before final judgment is rendered, to recover, instead of actual damages and profits, an award of statutory damages for all infringements involved in the action, with respect to any one work, for which any one infringer is liable individually, or for which any two or more infringers are liable jointly and severally, in a sum of not less than $750 or more than $30,000 as the court considers just. For the purposes of this subsection, all the parts of a compilation or derivative work constitute one work.

(2) In a case where the copyright owner sustains the burden of proving, and the court finds, that infringement was committed willfully, the court in its discretion may increase the award of statutory damages to a sum of not more than $150,000. In a case where the infringer sustains the burden of proving, and the court finds, that such infringer was not aware and had no reason to believe that his or her acts constituted an infringement of copyright, the court in its discretion may reduce the award of statutory damages to a sum of not less than $200. The court shall remit statutory damages in any case where an infringer believed and had reasonable grounds for believing that his or her use of the copyrighted work was a fair use under section 107, if the infringer was: (i) an employee or agent of a nonprofit educational institution, library, or archives acting within the scope of his or her employment who, or such institution, library, or archives itself, which infringed by reproducing the work in copies or phonorecords; or (ii) a public broadcasting entity which or a person who, as a regular part of the nonprofit activities of a public broadcasting entity (as defined in subsection (g) of section 118) infringed by performing a published nondramatic literary work or by reproducing a transmission program embodying a performance of such a work.

[Section 504 continues with other specific provisions about monetary liabilities that are generally not important to the work of educators or librarians.]

Section 1201. Circumvention of Copyright Protection Systems

(a) VIOLATIONS REGARDING CIRCUMVENTION OF TECHNOLOGICAL MEASURES.—

(1)(A) No person shall circumvent a technological measure that effectively controls access to a work protected under this title. The prohibition contained in the preceding sentence shall take effect at the end of the 2-year period beginning on the date of the enactment of this chapter.

(B) The prohibition contained in subparagraph (A) shall not apply to persons who are users of a copyrighted work which is in a particular class of works, if such persons are, or are likely to be in the succeeding 3-year period, adversely affected by virtue of such prohibition in their ability to make noninfringing uses of that particular class of works under this title, as determined under subparagraph (C).

[Section 1201 continues with details about the authority of the Librarian of Congress to create exceptions to the anticircumvention provision. The statute also includes lengthy and elaborate statutory exceptions.]

B Checklist for Fair Use

Prepared by the Copyright Management Center
Indiana University–Purdue University Indianapolis

We are pleased to offer the following "Checklist for Fair Use" as a helpful tool for the academic community. We hope that it will serve two purposes. First, it should help educators, librarians, and others to focus on factual circumstances that are important to the evaluation of a contemplated fair use of copyrighted works. A reasonable fair-use analysis is based on four factors set forth in the fair-use provision of copyright law, Section 107 of the Copyright Act of 1976. The application of those factors depends on the particular facts of your situation, and changing one or more facts may alter the outcome of the analysis. The "Checklist for Fair Use" derives from those four factors and from the judicial decisions interpreting copyright law.

A second purpose of the checklist is to provide an important means for recording your decision-making process. Maintaining a record of your fair-use analysis is critical to establishing your "reasonable and good-faith" attempts to apply fair use to meet your educational objectives. Section 504(c)(2) of the Copyright Act offers some protection for educators and librarians who act in good faith. Once you have completed your application of fair use to a particular need, keep your completed checklist in your files for future reference.

As you use the checklist and apply it to your situation, you are likely to check more than one box in each column and even check boxes across columns. Some checked boxes will "favor fair use," and others may "oppose fair use." A key concern is whether you are acting reasonably in checking any given box; the ultimate concern is whether the cumulative "weight" of the factors favors or opposes fair use. Because you are most familiar with your project, you are probably best positioned to make that decision. To learn more about fair use and other aspects of copyright law, visit the Copyright Management Center website at http://www.copyright.iupui.edu.

Checklist for Fair Use

Name: _____ Date: _____ Project: _____

Institution: _____ Prepared by: _____

PURPOSE

Favoring Fair Use

☐ Teaching (including multiple copies for classroom use)

☐ Research

☐ Scholarship

☐ Nonprofit educational institution

☐ Criticism

☐ Comment

☐ News reporting

☐ Transformative or productive use (changes the work for new utility)

☐ Restricted access (to students or other appropriate group)

☐ Parody

Opposing Fair Use

☐ Commercial activity

☐ Profiting from the use

☐ Entertainment

☐ Bad-faith behavior

☐ Denying credit to original author

NATURE

Favoring Fair Use

☐ Published work

☐ Factual or nonfiction-based

☐ Important to favored educational objectives

Opposing Fair Use

☐ Unpublished work

☐ Highly creative work (art, music, novels, films, plays)

☐ Fiction

AMOUNT

Favoring Fair Use

☐ Small quantity

☐ Portion used is not central or significant to entire work

☐ Amount is appropriate for favored educational purpose

Opposing Fair Use

☐ Large portion or whole work used

☐ Portion used is central to the work or is the "heart of the work"

EFFECT

Favoring Fair Use

☐ User owns lawfully acquired or purchased copy of original work

☐ One or few copies made

☐ No significant effect on the market or potential market for copyrighted work

☐ No similar product marketed by the copyright holder

☐ Lack of licensing mechanism

Opposing Fair Use

☐ Could replace sale of copyrighted work

☐ Significantly impairs market or potential market for copyrighted work or derivative

☐ Reasonably available licensing mechanism for use of the copyrighted work

☐ Affordable permission available for using work

☐ Numerous copies made

☐ You made it accessible on the Internet or in other public forum

☐ Repeated or long-term use

C Checklist for the TEACH Act

Prepared by the Copyright Management Center
Indiana University–Purdue University Indianapolis

Background of the Law

Congress enacted the TEACH Act in 2002 to address issues surrounding lawful uses of copyrighted works in distance education. The act is a full revision of Section 110(2) of the U.S. Copyright Act, and it allows educators to use certain copyrighted works in distance education without permission from, or payment of royalties to, the copyright owner. By complying with the law, users can be protected from copyright infringements. The TEACH Act improves upon previous law by allowing uses of an expanded range of works in distance education. In particular, educators may now make performances of nondramatic literary or musical works in full and performances of portions of any other works; educators may also make displays of works in an amount comparable to that which is typically displayed in the course of a live classroom session. The challenge of the TEACH Act is the numerous conditions and requirements for compliance. Educators must satisfy all requirements of the law in order to enjoy its benefits.

Purpose of the Checklist

The primary purpose of this checklist is to help document your compliance with the TEACH Act. The checklist enumerates the law's many requirements and groups them according to the unit within the educational institution that will likely be responsible for each step. We suggest that educators complete and keep a copy of this document in connection with each distance-education course. Maintaining such records may be critical for demonstrating your compliance. This checklist may also be an effective planning or teaching tool, fostering an understanding of the law's detailed requirements.

For More Information

For more information about the TEACH Act and about fair use, permissions, and other copyright issues applicable to distance education, please visit the website of the Copyright Management Center at http://www.copyright.iupui.edu.

Checklist for the TEACH Act

Name: _____ Date: _____ Project: _____

Institution: _____ Prepared by: _____

TEACH Act requirements that will likely fall within the duty of the *instructor*:

1. The work to be transmitted may be any of the following:
   - ☐ A performance of a nondramatic literary work; or
   - ☐ A performance of a nondramatic musical work; or
   - ☐ A performance of any other work, including dramatic works and audiovisual works, but only in "reasonable and limited portions"; or
   - ☐ A display in an amount comparable to that which is typically displayed in the course of a live classroom session.

2. The work to be transmitted may not be any of the following:
   - ☐ Marketed primarily for performance or display as part of a digitally transmitted mediated instructional activity; or
   - ☐ A textbook, coursepack, or other material in any media which is typically purchased or acquired by students for their independent use and retention.

3. Any permitted performance or display must be both:
   - ☐ Made by, at the direction of, or under the actual supervision of an instructor as an integral part of a class session offered as a regular part of the systematic, mediated instructional activities of the educational institution; and
   - ☐ Directly related and of material assistance to the teaching content of the transmission.

4. The institution does not know or have reason to believe that the copy of the work to be transmitted was not lawfully made or acquired.

5. If the work to be used has to be converted from print or another analog version to digital format, then both:
   - ☐ The amount of the work converted is no greater than the amount that can lawfully be used for the course; and
   - ☐ There is no digital version of the work available to the institution or the digital version available to the institution has technological protection that prevents its lawful use for the course.

TEACH ACT requirements that will likely fall within the duty of the *institution*:

6. The institution for which the work is transmitted is an accredited nonprofit educational institution.

7. The institution has instituted policies regarding copyright.

8. The institution has provided information materials to faculty, students, and relevant staff members that describe and promote U.S. copyright laws.

9. The institution has provided notice to students that materials used in connection with the course may be subject to copyright protection.

10. The transmission of the content is made solely for students officially enrolled in the course for which the transmission is made.

TEACH Act requirements that will likely fall within the duty of the *information technology officials*:

11. Technological measures have been taken to reasonably prevent both:
    - ☐ Retention of the work in accessible form by students for longer than the class session; and
    - ☐ Unauthorized further dissemination of the work in accessible form by such recipients to others.

12. The institution has not engaged in conduct that could reasonably be expected to interfere with technological measures used by copyright owners to prevent retention or dissemination of their works.

13. The work is stored on a system or network in a manner that is ordinarily not accessible to anyone other than anticipated recipients.

14. The copy of the work will only be maintained on the system or network in a manner ordinarily accessible for a period that is reasonably necessary to facilitate the transmissions for which it was made.

15. Any copies made for the purpose of transmitting the work are retained and used solely by the institution.

D Model Letter for Permission Requests

The following letter is offered as guidance for drafting letters to copyright owners when permission to use the work is necessary This letter should be revised to meet your particular needs. Always keep a copy of the letter for your records.

[Date]

[Letterhead or return address]

[Rights holder name and address]

Dear [Sir or Madam] [Permissions Editor] [Personal name, if known]:

I am in the process of creating [Describe project]. I would like your permission to include the following material with this [Project]:

[Citation with source information]

The [Project and material] will be used [Describe how the project and material will be used]. It will be accessible by [Describe users].

If you do not control the copyright on all of the above-mentioned material, I would appreciate any contact information you can give me regarding the proper rights holder(s), including current address(es). Otherwise, your permission confirms that you hold the right to grant the permission requested here.

I would greatly appreciate your consent to my request. If you require any additional information, please do not hesitate to contact me. I can be reached at:

[Your contact information]

A duplicate copy of this request has been provided for your records. If you agree with the terms as described above, please sign the permission form below and send one copy with the self-addressed return envelope I have provided.

Sincerely,

[Signature]

[Typed name]

Permission granted for the use of the material as described above:

Agreed to: _____ Name and Title: _____

Company/Affiliation: _____ Date:_____

GUIDE TO ADDITIONAL READING

Multivolume Treatises

Goldstein, Paul. *Copyright*. 2nd ed. 4 vols. Boston: Little, Brown, 2004.

Nimmer, Melville B., and David Nimmer. *Nimmer on Copyright*. 10 vols. New York: Matthew Bender, 2005.

Copyright Law: Practical Understanding and Application

Andorka, Frank H. *What Is a Copyright?* 2nd ed. Chicago: American Bar Association, Section of Intellectual Property Law, 2001.

Elias, Stephen. *Patent, Copyright and Trademark: A Desk Reference to Intellectual Property Law*. 7th ed. Berkeley, CA: Nolo, 2004.

Fishman, Stephen. *The Copyright Handbook: How to Protect and Use Written Works*. 8th ed. Berkeley, CA: Nolo, 2004.

Jasper, Margaret. *The Law of Copyright*. Dobbs Ferry, NY: Oceana, 2000.

Leaffer, Marshall. *Understanding Copyright Law*. 4th ed. New York: Matthew Bender, 2004.

Samuels, Edward. *The Illustrated Story of Copyright*. New York: Thomas Dunne Books, St. Martin's Press, 2000.

Stim, Richard. *Copyright Law*. Albany, NY: West Legal Studies, 2000.

Strong, William S. *The Copyright Book: A Practical Guide*. 5th ed. Cambridge, MA: MIT Press, 1999.

Copyright Law: Policy and Concepts

Goldstein, Paul. *Copyright's Highway: The Law and Lore of Copyright from Gutenberg to the Celestial Jukebox*. Rev. ed. Stanford, CA: Stanford Law and Politics, 2003.

Lessig, Lawrence. *Code and Other Laws of Cyberspace*. New York: Basic Books, 1999.

———. *The Future of Ideas: The Fate of the Commons in a Connected World*. New York: Random House, 2001.

Nimmer, David. *Copyright: Sacred Text, Technology, and the DMCA*. The Hague: Kluwer Law International, 2003.

Patterson, Lyman Ray. *Copyright in Historical Perspective*. Nashville, TN: Vanderbilt University Press, 1968.

Patterson, L. Ray, and Stanley W. Lindberg. *The Nature of Copyright: A Law of Users' Rights*. Athens: University of Georgia Press, 1991.

Saint-Amour, Paul K. *The Copywrights: Intellectual Property and the Literary Imagination*. Ithaca, NY: Cornell University Press, 2003.

Vaidhanathan, Siva. *Copyrights and Copywrongs: The Rise of Intellectual Property and How It Threatens Creativity*. New York: New York University Press, 2001.

Copyright for Librarianship and Education

Banis, Robert J. *Copyright Issues for Librarians, Teachers and Authors*. 2nd ed. Chesterfield, MO: Science and Humanities, 2001.

Besek, June M. *Copyright Issues Relevant to the Creation of a Digital Archive: A Preliminary Assessment*. Washington, DC: Council on Library Information Resources, Library of Congress, 2003.

Bruwelheide, Janis H. *The Copyright Primer for Librarians and Educators*. 2nd ed. Chicago and Washington, DC: American Library Association, National Education Association, 1995.

Butler, Rebecca P. *Copyright for Teachers and Librarians*. New York: Neal-Schuman, 2004.

Croft, Janet Brennan. *Legal Solutions in Electronic Reserves and the Electronic Delivery of Interlibrary Loan.* New York: Haworth Information, 2005.

Driscoll, Lori. *Electronic Reserve: A Manual for Library Staff Members.* New York: Haworth Information, 2003.

Gasaway, Laura N., and Sarah K. Wiant. *Libraries and Copyright: A Guide to Copyright Law in the 1990s.* Washington, DC: Special Libraries Association, 1994.

Harper, Georgia K. *Copyright Issues in Higher Education.* 2nd ed. Washington, DC: National Association of College and University Attorneys, 2001.

Harris, Lesley. *Licensing Digital Content: A Practical Guide for Librarians.* Chicago: American Library Association, 2002.

Lipinski, Tomas A. *Copyright Law and the Distance Education Classroom.* Lanham, MD: Scarecrow, 2005.

Minow, Mary, and Tomas A. Lipinski. *The Library's Legal Answer Book.* Chicago: American Library Association, 2003.

Monotti, Ann Louise. *Universities and Intellectual Property: Ownership and Exploitation.* Oxford: Oxford University Press, 2003.

Padfield, Timothy. *Copyright for Archivists and Users of Archives.* 2nd ed. London: Facet, 2004.

Rosedale, Jeff, ed. *Managing Electronic Reserves.* Chicago: American Library Association, 2002.

Russell, Carrie. *Complete Copyright: An Everyday Guide for Librarians.* Chicago: American Library Association, 2004.

Simpson, Carol Mann. *Copyright for Schools: A Practical Guide.* 3rd ed. Worthington, OH: Linworth, 2001.

Talab, R. S. *Commonsense Copyright: A Guide for Educators and Librarians.* Jefferson, NC: McFarland, 1999.

Wherry, Timothy Lee. *The Librarian's Guide to Intellectual Property in the Digital Age: Copyrights, Patents, and Trademarks.* Chicago: American Library Association, 2002.

Permission from Copyright Owners

Jassin, Lloyd J. *The Copyright Permission and Libel Handbook: A Step-by-Step Guide for Writers, Editors, and Publishers.* New York: Wiley, 1998.

Stim, Richard. *Getting Permission: How to License and Clear Copyrighted Materials Online and Off.* 2nd ed. Berkeley, CA: Nolo, 2004.

Eligibility of Works for Protection

Boyd, Steven S. "Deriving Originality in Derivative Works: Considering the Quantum of Originality Needed to Attain Copyright Protection in a Derivative Work." *Santa Clara Law Review* 40 (2000): 325–78.

Durham, Alan L. "Speaking of the World: Fact, Opinion and the Originality Standard of Copyright." *Arizona State Law Journal* 33 (Fall 2001): 791–848.

Gervais, Daniel J. "Feist Goes Global: A Comparative Analysis of the Notion of Originality." *Journal of the Copyright Society of the U.S.A.* 49 (Summer 2002): 949–81.

Copyright Duration

Bard, Robert L., and Lewis Kurlantzick. *Copyright Duration: Duration, Term Extension, the European Union and the Making of Copyright Policy.* San Francisco: Austin and Winfield, 1999.

Crews, Kenneth D. "Copyright Duration and the Progressive Degeneration of a Constitutional Doctrine." *Syracuse Law Review* 55 (2005): 189–250.

Gasaway, Laura N. *When Works Pass into the Public Domain.* Available from http://www.unc.edu/~unclng/public-d.htm.

Hirtle, Peter B. "Copyright Term and the Public Domain in the United States." Available from http://www.copyright.cornell.edu/training/Hirtle_Public_Domain.htm.

Ochoa, Tyler T. "Patent and Copyright Term Extension and the Constitution: A Historical Perspective." *Journal of the Copyright Society of the U.S.A.* 49 (Fall 2001): 19–125.

Public Domain

Fishman, Stephen. *The Public Domain: How to Find Copyright-Free Writings, Music, Art and More.* 2nd ed. Berkeley, CA: Nolo, 2004.

Martin, Scott M. "The Mythology of the Public Domain: Exploring the Myths behind Attacks on the Duration of Copyright Protection." *Loyola of Los Angeles Law Review* 36 (Fall 2002): 253–322.

Zimmerman, Barbara. *The Mini-Encyclopedia of Public Domain Songs.* New York: BZ Rights Stuff, 1999.

Copyright Ownership

Franklin, Janice R. *Database Ownership and Copyright Issues among Automated Library Networks: An Analysis and Case Study*. Norwood, NJ: Ablex, 1993.

Gasaway, Laura N. "Copyright Ownership and The Impact on Academic Libraries." *DePaul-LCA Journal of Art and Entertainment Law* 13 (Fall 2003): 277–311.

Geller, Paul Edward. "Conflicts of Laws in Copyright Cases: Infringement and Ownership Issues." *Journal of the Copyright Society of the U.S.A.* 51 (Winter 2004): 315–94.

Holmes, Georgia, and Daniel A. Levin. "Who Owns Course Materials Prepared by a Teacher or Professor? The Application of Copyright Law to Teaching Materials in the Internet Age." *Brigham Young University Education and Law Journal* (2000): 165–89.

Johnson, Andrea L. "Reconciling Copyright Ownership Policies for Faculty-Authors in Distance Education." *Journal of Law and Education* 33 (October 2004): 431–55.

Klein, Michael W. "'The Equitable Rule': Copyright Ownership of Distance Education Courses." *Journal of College and University Law* 31 (2004): 143–92.

Litman, Jessica. *Digital Copyright*. Amherst, NY: Prometheus Books, 2001.

McLeod, Kembrew. *Owning Culture: Authorship, Ownership, and Intellectual Property Law*. New York: P. Lang, 2001.

McSherry, Corynne. *Who Owns Academic Work? Battling for Control of Intellectual Property*. Cambridge, MA: Harvard University Press, 2001.

Slaughter, Sheila. *Academic Capitalism and the New Economy: Markets, State, and Higher Education*. Baltimore: Johns Hopkins University Press, 2004.

Townsend, Elizabeth. "Legal and Policy Responses to the Disappearing 'Teacher Exception,' or Copyright Ownership in the 21st Century University." *Minnesota Intellectual Property Review* 4 (2003): 209–83.

Exceptions to the Rights of Copyright Owners

Patry, William F. *The Fair Use Privilege in Copyright Law*. 2nd ed. Washington, DC: Bureau of National Affairs, 1995.

Seltzer, Leon E. *Exemptions and Fair Use in Copyright*. Cambridge, MA: Harvard University Press, 1978.

Senftleben, Martin. *Copyright, Limitations and the Three-Step Test: An Analysis of the Three-Step Test in International and EC Copyright Law*. The Hague: Kluwer Law International, 2004.

Fair-Use Guidelines

Crews, Kenneth D. "Fair Use and Higher Education: Are Guidelines the Answer?" *Academe* 83 (November–December 1997): 38–40.

———. "The Law of Fair Use and the Illusion of Fair-Use Guidelines." *Ohio State Law Journal* 62 (2001): 599–702.

Crews, Kenneth D., and Dwayne K. Buttler, eds. "Copyright and Fair-Use Guidelines for Education and Libraries." *Journal of the American Society for Information Science* 50 (December 1999): 1303–57.

Copyright and New Technology

Bielefield, Arlene. *Technology and Copyright Law: A Guidebook for the Library, Research, and Teaching Professions: 1999 Update*. New York: Neal-Schuman, 1999.

Dixon, Rod. *Open Source Software Law*. Boston: Artech House, 2004.

Fishman, Stephen. *Web and Software Development: A Legal Guide*. 3rd ed. Berkeley, CA: Nolo, 2002.

Hoffmann, Gretchen McCord. *Copyright in Cyberspace: Questions and Answers for Librarians*. New York: Neal-Schuman, 2001.

Hollaw, Lee A. *Legal Protection of Digital Information*. Washington, DC: Bureau of National Affairs, 2002.

Kasdorf, William E. *The Columbia Guide to Digital Publishing*. New York: Columbia University Press, 2003.

Koelling, Jill Marie. *Digital Imaging: A Practical Approach*. Walnut Creek, CA: AltaMira, 2004.

National Research Council, Committee on Intellectual Property Rights and the Emerging Information Infrastructure. *The Digital Dilemma: Intellectual Property in the Information Age*. Washington, DC: National Academy, 2000.

Rodríguez Pardo, Julián. *Copyright and Multimedia*. The Hague, New York: Kluwer Law International, 2003.

Rose, Lance. *Netlaw: Your Rights in the Online World.* Berkeley, CA: McGraw-Hill, 1995.

Tennant, Roy. *Managing the Digital Library.* New York: Reed, 2004.

Woo, Jisuk. *Copyright Law and Computer Programs: The Role of Communication in Legal Structure.* New York: Garland, 2000.

Copyright and Music

Althouse, Jay. *Copyright: The Complete Guide for Music Educators.* 2nd ed. Van Nuys, CA: Alfred, 1997.

Campana, Deborah. *Music Library Instruction.* Lanham, MD: Scarecrow, 2004.

Fisher, William W. *Promises to Keep: Technology, Law, and the Future of Entertainment.* Stanford, CA: Stanford Law and Politics, 2004.

Frith, Simon, and Lee Marshall, eds. *Music and Copyright.* 2nd ed. New York: Routledge, 2004.

Kohn, Al. *Kohn on Music Licensing.* 3rd ed. New York: Aspen Law and Business, 2002.

Lupo, Anthony V. *Music on the Internet: Understanding the New Rights and Solving New Problems.* New York: Practising Law Institute, 2001.

Stim, Richard. *Music Law: How to Run Your Band's Business.* 4th ed. Berkeley, CA: Nolo, 2004.

CASES CITED

A&M Records, Inc. v. Napster, Inc., 239 F.3d 1004 (9th Cir. 2001).

American Geophysical Union v. Texaco Inc., 60 F.3d 913 (2d Cir. 1994), *cert. dismissed*, 516 U.S. 1005 (1995).

Avtec Systems, Inc. v. Peiffer, 21 F.3d 568 (4th Cir. 1994).

Basic Books, Inc. v. Kinko's Graphics Corp., 758 F. Supp. 1522 (S.D.N.Y. 1991).

Basic Books, Inc. v. Kinko's Graphics Corp., 21 U.S.P.Q.2d 1639 (1991).

Bellsouth Advertising & Publishing Corp. v. Donnelley Information Publishing, Inc., 999 F.2d 1436 (11th Cir. 1993).

Bridgeman Art Library, Ltd. v. Corel Corp., 36 F. Supp. 2d 191 (S.D.N.Y. 1999).

Brown v. Ames, 201 F.3d 654 (5th Cir. 2000).

Burrow-Giles Lithographic Co. v. Sarony, 111 U.S. 53 (1884).

Campbell v. Acuff-Rose Music, Inc., 510 U.S. 569 (1994).

CDN Inc. v. Kapes, 197 F.3d 1256 (9th Cir. 1999).

Chamberlain Group, Inc. v. Skylink Technologies, Inc., 381 F.3d 1178 (Fed. Cir. 2004).

Chavez v. Arte Publico Press, 204 F.3d 601 (5th Cir. 2000).

Community for Creative Non-Violence v. Reid, 490 U.S. 730 (1989).

Eldred v. Ashcroft, 537 U.S. 186 (2003).

Elvis Presley Enterprises, Inc. v. Passport Video, 349 F.3d 622 (9th Cir. 2003).

Encyclopaedia Britannica Educational Corp. v. Crooks, 542 F. Supp. 1156 (W.D.N.Y. 1982).

Erickson v. Trinity Theatre, Inc., 202 F.3d 1227 (7th Cir. 1994).

Estate of Martin Luther King, Jr., Inc. v. CBS, Inc., 194 F.3d 1211 (11th Cir. 1999).

Feist Publications, Inc. v. Rural Telephone Service Co., 499 U.S. 340 (1991).

Folsom v. Marsh, 9 F. Cas. 171 (C.C. Mass. 1841).

Forasté v. Brown University, 248 F. Supp. 2d 71 (D.R.I. 2003).

Gaiman v. McFarlane, 360 F.3d 644 (7th Cir. 2004).

Harper & Row Publishers, Inc. v. Nation Enterprises, 471 U.S. 539 (1985).

Higgins v. Detroit Educational Broadcasting Foundation, 4 F. Supp. 2d 701 (E.D. Mich. 1998).

Infinity Broadcasting Corp. v. Kirkwood, 63 F. Supp. 2d 420 (S.D.N.Y. 1999).

Kelly v. Arriba Soft Corp., 336 F.3d 811 (9th Cir. 2003).

Lexmark International, Inc. v. Static Control Components, Inc., 387 F.3d 522 (6th Cir. 2004).

Los Angeles Times v. Free Republic, 54 U.S.P.Q.2d 1862 (C.D. Cal. 2000).

MAI Systems Corp. v. Peak Computer, Inc., 991 F.2d 511 (9th Cir. 1993).

Manning v. Parkland College, 109 F. Supp. 2d 976 (C.D. Ill. 2000).

Marcus v. Rowley, 695 F.2d 1171 (9th Cir. 1983).

Martin v. Indianapolis, 982 F. Supp. 625 (S.D. Ind. 1997), *aff'd*, 192 F.3d 608 (7th Cir. 1999).

Mattel, Inc. v. Walking Mountain Productions, 353 F.3d 792 (9th Cir. 2004).

Matthew Bender & Co. v. West Publishing Co., 158 F.3d 693 (2d Cir. 1998).

Maxtone-Graham v. Burtchaell, 803 F.2d 1253 (2d Cir. 1986), *cert. denied*, 481 U.S. 1059 (1987).

Metro-Goldwyn-Mayer Studios, Inc. v. Grokster, Ltd., 75 U.S.P.Q.2d 1001.

New Era Publications International v. Henry Holt and Co., 695 F. Supp. 1493 (S.D.N.Y. 1988), *aff'd*, 873 F.2d 576 (2d Cir. 1989).

NXIVM Corp. v. Ross Institute, 364 F.3d 471 (2d Cir. 2004).

Penelope v. Brown, 792 F. Supp. 132 (D. Mass. 1992).

Playboy v. Hardenburgh, 982 F. Supp. 503 (N.D. Ohio 1997).

Princeton University Press v. Michigan Document Services, Inc., 99 F.3d 1381 (6th Cir. 1996), *cert. denied*, 520 U.S. 1156 (1997).

Religious Technology Center v. NETCOM, 907 F. Supp. 1361 (N.D. Cal. 1995).

Ringgold v. Black Entertainment Television, Inc., 126 F.3d 70 (2d Cir. 1997).

Robert Stigwood Group Ltd. v. Sperber, 457 F.2d 50, 55 n.6 (2d Cir. 1972).

Salinger v. Random House, Inc., 811 F.2d 90 (2d Cir. 1987).

Sandoval v. New Line Cinema Corp., 147 F.3d 215 (2d Cir. 1998).

Shady Records, Inc. v. Source Enterprises, Inc., 2005 WL 14920 (S.D.N.Y. 2005).

Silverstein v. Penguin Putnam, Inc., 368 F.3d 77 (2d Cir. 2005).

Sony Computer Entertainment America Inc. v. Gamemasters, 87 F. Supp. 2d 976 (N.D. Cal. 1999).

Sony Computer Entertainment, Inc. v. Connectix Corp., 203 F.3d 596 (9th Cir. 2000).

Sundeman v. Seajay Society, Inc., 142 F.3d 194 (4th Cir. 1998).

Tiffany Design, Inc. v. Reno-Tahoe Specialty, Inc., 55 F. Supp. 2d 1113 (D. Nev. 1999).

Universal City Studios, Inc. v. Reimerdes, 111 F. Supp. 2d 294 (S.D.N.Y. 2000), *aff'd sub nom. Universal City Studios, Inc. v. Corley*, 273 F.3d 429 (2d Cir. 2001).

University of Colorado Foundation, Inc. v. American Cyanamid, 880 F. Supp. 1387 (D. Colo. 1995).

U.S. v. Elcom, Ltd., 203 F. Supp. 2d 1111 (N.D. Cal. 2002).

Vanderhurst v. Colorado Mountain College Dist., 16 F. Supp. 2d 1297 (D. Colo. 1998).

Wright v. Warner Books, Inc., 953 F.2d 731 (2d Cir. 1991).

INDEX

KENNETH D. CREWS is the Samuel R. Rosen II Professor of Law and Director of the Center for Intellectual Property and Innovation at the Indiana University School of Law–Indianapolis, with a joint appointment to the Indiana University School of Library and Information Science. He is Associate Dean of the Faculties for Copyright Management and Director of the Copyright Management Center at Indiana University–Purdue University Indianapolis. Crews studied history at Northwestern University before receiving his law degree from Washington University in St. Louis. He practiced law in Los Angeles and earned master's and PhD degrees from UCLA's graduate School of Library and Information Science. His research centers on copyright and intellectual property issues of importance to educators and librarians. He is the author of *Copyright, Fair Use, and the Challenge for Universities* (1993), among other books. In 2005 the American Library Association awarded Crews the L. Ray Patterson Copyright Award: In Support of Users' Rights.